Rabbi Aft

With much gratitude.

Bruce & Phyllis Kaplan

Bruce + Phyllis Kaplan

June 5, 2003

10th grade confirmation, erev shavuot

Abraham and Sons

Seymour M. Panitz

DEVORA PUBLISHING

Published by Devora Publishing

Cover Design: Ben Gasner
Book Design: Benjie Herskowitz

Cloth ISBN: 1-930143-27-3

Devora Publishing
40 East 78th Street, Suite 16D, New York, New York 10021
Tel: (800) 232-2931
Fax: (212) 472-6253
Email: pop@netvision.net.il
Website: www.pitspopany.com

Printed in Israel

In Loving Memory of
Our Parents

Ezekiel and Nettie Panitz
יחזקאל בן אברהם יעקב ורבקה
נחמה נעכע בת יצחק וביילה

Solomon and Rebecca Reisner
שלמה זלמן בן אברהם ישראל וריבה לאה
רבקה בת יחיאל הלוי ורייזע באשעל

Acknowledgments

No man is an island, and no idea exists in a vacuum. Charting an individual course does not diminish the debt that I (and all of us) owe to the enriching influence of the many who have creatively refined our understanding of the Book of Genesis. In this spirit I record my debt to the patient ear, enthusiastic comments and generous support of countless teachers, colleagues, friends and family members.

It was my parents, of blessed memory, who first opened my eyes to the rich source of guidance that is our Torah. Many teachers helped develop my appreciation for its message, and challenged me to pass it on to others. This work is my humble attempt to do so, in the spirit of *lilmod al m'nat l'lamed,* to study so as to be able to teach.

My brothers and sister (two of whom now abide in the Academy on High) gave me a model for sibling loyalty which helped me perceive it in Isaac and in Ishmael. My sister-in-law, Esther Panitz, was generous with advice on the fine points of the art of writing. From my children has come not only advice and support, but the model which helped illustrate for me the eternal truth, represented by Isaac and Ishmael, both sons of Abraham, that each child makes his or her own way in life, and that all are ways of truth, all acceptable in the sight of God.

To my beloved wife, Barbara, my thanks for many things. For the sure knowledge that home is a place to find peace of mind and quiet for the soul. For the encouragement which made this entire effort possible. For probing questions on the events and characters in Genesis which spurred me on to find one man's answer. And above all, for serving as a real-life paradigm of the unstinting loving and supportive loyalty which I have placed at the center of the relationship of Abraham and Sarah, and of Abraham and all his circle.

I am indebted to friends who provided technical resources, especially Samy Ymar. I particularly record here my thanks to Chaim Mazo, Ben Gasner and Benjie Herskowitz of the Devora Publishing staff, and especially to my editor, Yaacov Peterseil, for their efforts to help the book please both the inner and outer eye of the reader. For the text which greets the reader, I accept full responsibility.

Then Abraham died, after a full and satisfying life, at a ripe old age.

And his sons Isaac and Ishmael buried him in the cave of Machpelah.

Genesis 25: 8-9

Major Characters

Abraham, (Abram), traditionally recognized as the discoverer of the One God

Sarah, (Sarai), his wife, mother of Isaac, partner in his dream of propagating the message of the One God

Isaac, Abraham's son, who continued the Biblical line of succession that developed into the Jewish People

Ishmael, actually Abraham's first-born, identified by many as the ancestor of the Arab peoples

Hagar, Sarah's handmaiden, mother of Ishmael

Eliezer, Abraham's right-hand man, and narrator of parts of this book

Minor characters include Abraham's father **Terah,** his brother **Nahor,** his nephew **Lot,** Hagar's father **Locum-Re,** and Abraham's second wife **Keturah**

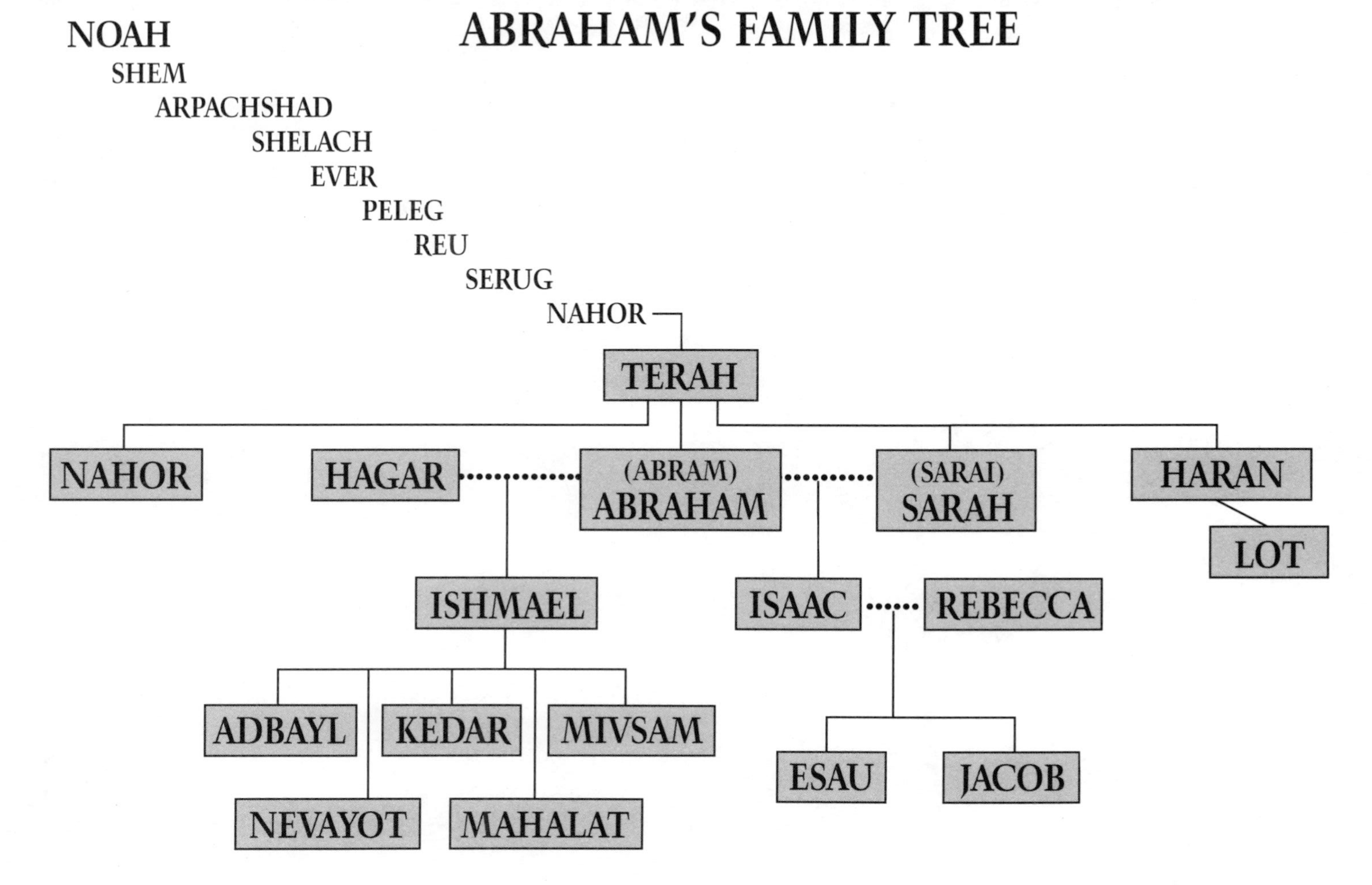

ABRAHAM'S FAMILY TREE
NOAH
SHEM
ARPACHSHAD
SHELACH
EVER
PELEG
REU
SERUG
NAHOR
TERAH
NAHOR
HAGAR
(ABRAM) ABRAHAM
(SARAI) SARAH
HARAN
LOT
ISHMAEL
ISAAC
REBECCA
ADBAYL
KEDAR
MIVSAM
NEVAYOT
MAHALAT
ESAU
JACOB

TIME LINE

AGE		EVENT	BIBLICAL REFERENCE
Reu	Abram		
1		Reu born (son of Peleg / grandson of Ever)	Gen 11:18
32		Reu begets Serug	Gen 11:20
62		Serug begets Nahor (age 30)	Gen 11:22
91		Nahor begets Terah (age 29)	Gen 11:24
161	1	Terah 'begets Abram, Nahor and Haran' (age 70)	Gen 11:26
171	11	Sarai born (Terah's age 80; Abram's age 10)	
189	28	Abram & Sarai married	
210	49	Nahor dies	Gen 11:25
211	50	Terah, Abram, Sarai & Lot leave Ur	
236	75	Abram and family arrive in Canaan	Gen 12:4
239	78	Reu dies (age 239)	Gen 11:21
		Abram and Sarai in Egypt	Gen 12:9-21
		Abram 'rescues' Lot;	
		saves Sodom and four additional cities	Gen 14
		Abram's Vision	Gen 15
246	85	Abram takes Hagar 'as wife'	Gen 16:3
247	86	Ishmael born	Gen 17:24-25
260	99	Abram's second vision;	
		Abram renamed Abraham	Gen 17
	99	Destruction of Sodom / Adventures of Lot	Gen 18
	99	Abraham 'bargains' with God	Gen 18
261	100	Isaac born (Sarah's age 90)	Gen 21:5
262	101	Serug dies (age 230)	Gen 11:23
263	102	Hagar and Ishmael banished	
		(Isaac's age 2; Ishmael's age 16)	Gen 21:9-21
277	116	Akeda (Isaac's age 16; Ishmael's age 30)	Gen 22:1-19
296	135	Terah dies (age 205)	Gen 11: 22
298	137	Sarah dies, (age 127)	
		(Isaac's age 37; Ishmael's age 51)	Gen 23:1
	140	Isaac marries Rebecca (Isaac's age 40)	Gen 25:20
	160	Jacob and Esau born (Isaac's age 60)	Gen 25:25-26
	175	Abraham dies; buried by sons Isaac and Ishmael	
		(Isaac's age 75; Ishmael's age 90)	Gen 25:7-9

FOREWORD

In another day, I would have prefaced this work with an imaginative account of a discovery by a participant in the Six Day War of an old, yellowed manuscript, somewhere deep in the Sinai Peninsula. Or I might have written of a mythical ancient Midrash, uncovered in some long-forgotten out-of-the-way Genizah. I decided against any such fiction. Quite the contrary: I admit with some pride to having set down on paper a highly personal reading of a series of Biblical events.

This book had its conception in the words of Genesis 25: 8-9, which spoke to me in a new voice one fine Shabbat morning.

> *Then Abraham died, after a full and satisfying life,*
> *at a ripe old age. And his sons Isaac and Ishmael*
> *buried him in the cave of Machpelah.*

'What?' I asked myself, 'Ishmael came to the funeral of the same Abraham who had put him out of the family home! Isaac knew where to reach him! Isaac expected him to come!'

More questions followed, and, as I kept asking, I was left with no doubt that the way I had always understood many events narrated in chapters 11 through 25 of the Book of Genesis needed to be rethought. Specifically, as a starter, that account of the banishment of Ishmael and Hagar. I read on, with these questions resonating in my mind. It became clear to me that much of the Biblical record called out for a similar fresh look. It was obvious to me, as well, that a scant fifteen chapters leaves out much more of what happened than it preserves. I looked for more between the lines, and found more. As I brought events into focus, I fleshed out the characters of Abraham, Sarah, Hagar, Isaac and Ishmael; I have added that of Eliezer.

From the beginning, several alternatives were open to me.

I could have made a thorough study of the wealth of rabbinic material concerning Abraham and his offspring. I did not.

I could have taken a comprehensive look at the abundance of current interpretations of the Book of Genesis and its parts. I did not.

I could have immersed myself in the rich literature of structured theological investigation. I did not.

What then have I done? With full appreciation for what minds and learning greater than mine have created, I decided to set down a record highlighting what I myself have added to the lines of the Biblical narrative. From one point of view, it follows in the mainstream of a classical Jewish approach to revealing what lies beneath the surface of the Biblical text as written. It is known as *Midrash*. There are many midrashim, with frequently competing views; recent readings in this tradition are labelled *modern midrash*. In a very real sense, though, since much of the resultant work is a series of additions, one might call *Abraham and Sons* fiction, and speculative fiction at that. I hope not only that the book here presented is interesting reading, but that it contains food for thought as well.

Every literary work starts with certain presuppositions. My first flows from the view, axiomatic to Judaism, that it is to Abraham that we owe our understanding that there is but One God. It follows, to my mind, that Abraham was as perceptive as we are of ethical truth and as loyal to its dictates. In our day we have concluded that a compassionate and righteous God cannot have desired to see Isaac consumed by flames on the altar; Abraham *must* have seen this before us, and acted accordingly. In my humble opinion this truth is among many that are ours because of what Abraham taught the world. My reading of the Akedah, as well as that of the sudden departure of Ishmael and Hagar from Abraham's household, accepts this 'bias' and goes on from there.

A second point. An instinctive first reaction to a number of episodes in the life of Abraham is to ask: 'How could he!?'

> *How could Abraham have exposed his wife to the Pharaoh's sexual passion?*
>
> *How could he have ejected his first-born Ishmael and Hagar from his home?*
>
> *How could he have even considered the sacrifice of his son Isaac?*

To ask 'What could have happened to Abraham?' begs the question. I, for my part, have come to feel that the real question is, 'What was really going on? What lies just beneath the surface?' In other words: *Find the context*. I hope that I have.

A final point is that I extend *de facto* acceptance to that which the Biblical text presents to us. Thus, I take as factual Abraham's statement (Genesis 20:12) that he and Sarah are half-brother and half-sister. It helps add depth to my account. Likewise, I accept as grounded in fact the various ages and life spans as related to us: if nothing else, they make for interesting overlaps of lives. My Time Line, which frames the Biblical references numerically, and my Family Tree may also be helpful to the reader.

These and similar presuppositions highlight my reconstruction at every turn. My answers ring true to me; I hope that they do likewise for you, the reader.

A word about the mode of narration: It posits a series of letters to and from the major characters, excerpts from personal diaries, journals and other records, and entries in the files of Abraham's enterprises. It constantly shifts its point of view, and exposes for the reader the outlooks and priorities of each of the *dramatis personae* in turn. The narrative is carried along through a series of 'items' identified as to source, and numbered to suggest selection from a presumed comprehensive file, with intriguing gaps in the sequence of numbers. I could have divided it into a dozen or so chapters, but opted for this more fluid arrangement.

Our sages have taught us that the Torah may be interpreted in seventy ways. Perhaps mine is a seventy-first path. Perhaps it will win a place somewhat higher on the list. Perhaps at the end of the day it will be deemed out of place on the roster. You, the readers, will decide.

Daily we pray: *Praised be our Lord Who created us for His Glory ... May he open our hearts to His Torah*. In this vein I have labored, understanding all the while that the struggle to plumb the meaning of the Torah cannot reach its end with any one person's efforts, but that we are all duty-bound to continue it. I hope only that what I have 'recorded' here will help show the way to others to find meaning in God's word.

Finally, in closing, I turn to words that the Torah ascribes to Abraham's 'senior servant' whom we identify as Eliezer:

Blessed is the Lord, God of Abraham, who has guided me on the path to truth.

Dear Eliezer,

Abraham has died. An era has come to a close.

I doubt that humanity will ever again witness such a person. We might find many ways to describe his greatness; they all add up to one thing: He changed forever the way in which we think of God and of the relationship of human beings to God.

This, I am certain, will be his true, lasting memorial.

In accordance with Abraham's instructions, he was laid to rest alongside Sarah, his wife of one hundred and nine years. Things went smoothly, thanks to the full, deep brotherly understanding between Ishmael and Isaac.

The two of them stayed at Abraham's side as his health waned; during the last few days of his life they did not leave him.

In two touching tributes, they spoke lovingly of their father. Those who look for such things were disappointed not to hear even a whisper of resentment for certain acts of their father that may have upset them.

At the graveside, they walked shoulder to shoulder, followed close behind by Abraham's widow, Keturah.

At my prodding, they have done one more thing. They have given me permission to provide you with copies of items in the file in which you have a legitimate interest. As they agreed: 'It was his work that created it all.'

(There are even documents here of which no other copy exists.)

It is a sizable bundle, well over three hundred items in all. (I have numbered everything. Retain the numbers or not as you see fit.) A large part, I am sure, you will not keep. Yet, when the day is done, you will have a more comprehensive record of Abraham's years than exists in any other one place.

Thanks again, for trusting me to work with you and Abraham. The three of us worked well together. Now younger hands will take over.

Respectfully yours,

Yovav

ABRAHAM AND SONS

MOST OF MY FRIENDS HAVE
PARENTS AND

THINGS THAT ARE
EVERY-DAY MATTERS AS WELL AS
THINGS THAT ARE IMPORTANT.
I THINK I HAVE SEEN YOU TWICE IN MY
WHOLE LIFE, BUT I STILL REMEMBER TH
STORIES YOU TOLD ME ABOUT YOUR
GRANDFATHER EVER, ABOUT WHY P PLE
LEAVE ONE PLACE AND SETTLE IN ANO HER,
HOW PEOPLE DECIDE TO CALL SOME PL CE
"HOME," HOW FAMILIES GROW, AND HOW
IDEAS COME INTO MIND.
IT AMAZES ME HOW SOMETIMES THIN S
COME TOGETHER. TO BEGIN WITH, I M ST

ITEM # 1
LETTER FROM ABRAM TO REU

Dear Great-Great-Grandpa,

Most of my friends have their grandparents and great-grandparents close by, and it must be wonderful to be able to talk about things that are just everyday matters as well as things that are important.

I think I have seen you twice in my whole life, but I still remember the stories you told me about your grandfather Ever, about why people leave one place and settle in another, how people decide to call some place 'home,' how families grow, and how ideas come into our mind.

It amazes me how sometimes things come together. To begin with, I must remind you of another great-great-grandchild of yours, Sarai. She is only six, but she has a way of seeing things that no one else sees, she has a gift for expressing herself, and a talent for getting her way. Anyway, I was taking her for a walk in my favorite grove, and we came across a sort of open glen, one end sacred to the shepherds, and the area facing it sacred to the farmers. She just has to know everything, and so I explained the significance of the sacred tree, of the image of the god Marduk, of the spirit-in-the-spring, the divine grasses, the sun in the sky, the invisible moon and the stars, and of everything else. What she asked, I should have had the brains to ask: 'Isn't there just one person who makes all these things happen, and who makes them work together?' To me, once the question was asked, only one answer was possible: 'Yes.' To be sure, we then tried to nail down what we meant by 'person.'

That question stumped us both.

Once she led me to the magic phrase, 'One God,' wheels started turning in my mind. Who is this God? ... What are the limits of His (or Her) power? ... What does He want from us? ... How do we get to know Him? ... Does He have a physical form?

I, of course, am not a child of six, but a real man, sixteen years old. In an eerie sort of way, I grew up all at once on that day. My whole way of looking at the world changed, never to change back again, I am sure. Of course, I had a long list of questions, and as I have always done, I took them to Father.

He must have asked you all kinds of questions when he was young; I venture to say that Terah has the same mind-set now that he had growing up with you in Akkad. He is so deeply into his world of dozens of gods, represented by hundreds of forms, with no limit to how many idols and images we may make of them, that he does not really get the picture of what 'One God' means. Which is to say, I am on my own. Sarai does not completely fathom what it is that I am trying to think through, but at least she looks at me with a kind of absolute faith that says: 'You are trying to do something true and important, and I know you will succeed.' Right now, child that she is, she is the only human being in all of Ur in whom I can confide.

Great-Great-Grandpa, people here say, when Reu was here, he could always be relied on for advice. He was the favorite grandson of Ever, and learned all kinds of secret lore from him. Tell me, am I on the right track? Are these questions deserving of our time and energy? Can we ever find the answer? And also, please, give me an answer to a personal question. Am I really Sarai's brother?

You will understand why I am asking.

Your loving grandson,

Abram

ITEM # 2
LETTER FROM REU TO ABRAM

Dear Abram,

Your letter takes me back almost fifty years, to when I could have conversations with your father and grandfather and with my father and grandfather.

It is true what they say about Grandpa Ever. He was – sort of, still is – a very sensitive person, extremely spiritual by nature. He used to ask the sort of questions you have come up with. Thinking back, I recall a number of conversations when we were on the verge of answering: 'One God.' But we never did.

Just remember, Abram, what your mind and your heart have led you to may not be the only possible answer, certainly not the answer that rings true for most of the world. Speaking for myself, it is just as logical to look at the sun, for example, as possessed of divine, independent powers, and at each nation as being under the wing of its own god. Our local midwives, to pick one example, take it as a given that there is a goddess of childbirth to whom they must be beholden. This faith gives them strength when they need it; I for one am not ready to take that away from them. Nor am I ready to decide that you are right or that they are right.

But you are still young. As you grow older, gain more experience of life, learn what people need and deepen your understanding of yourself, you will be able to approach people with your novel idea. You sound as if you will never be happy until you have a community of believers around you – so more power to you.

In any event, never forget that your father and grandfather are neither villains nor fools. They are in harmony with a world that sees life as being influenced by a host of divine beings. Your father, for one, has built his life around helping people relate to such powers through the senses of sight and touch. In the world as we now know it, there are many people who seem to need this help. Are you prepared to change them, perhaps to destroy what they believe in? Are you ready to guide them to another outlook? It is an extremely tall order.

I may be able to help, though. When my grandfather, Ever, was in his prime, he gave me a scroll with all sorts of musings on this subject, among others. It would be nice if you could talk these thoughts out with him. I'll try to send you the scroll someday.

I think that I read your mind correctly about Sarai. You are still young, you know, and Sarai, for all her being gifted, is a mere child. Back off. Your question, nonetheless, deserves an answer. In our own family, there are a number of instances where men married women with the same father. There is a great deal of sentiment in favor of such a practice. I myself, to be honest, think it better not to permit marriages of people so close. I am not sure about first cousins, although that has a pretty widespread approval. Whatever you decide, I will back you up – but not for eight or ten years or so.

My dear Abram, I am impressed by the way your mind looks at what we know and is not afraid to give answers that no one else has given. Let me lay out a problem for you, of a completely different kind – on the surface.

If I get a letter to or from Ur once in a year or two, I am pleased. On the other hand, there is always some sort of caravan, or an independent team of two or three camels, making their way, sometimes across great distances, from point to point. It is impossible, as things stand now, to know when they depart, when they arrive and what they will be able to bring. Think of it, first of all, as a way of bringing together not divine powers (about them, I am afraid, human beings will always disagree) but human beings and their resources and needs.

And, if you can follow me, this kind of effort might dovetail with what you wrote about. You will not find many sympathetic ears in Akkad or Ur, but who knows what you may come across in Hamat, Damascus, Ugarit, far-off Canaan or distant places like Egypt. Because I am not convinced you are right does not mean that there are not minds that think like yours somewhere. To put it differently, because you have found no one around here who shares your answers (or even your questions) you have to go that much further afield to discover such people and minds. But it will take some looking, and then more than a little convincing and testing.

You will forgive me, but I have taken these last two years since you wrote to fill in what I know of you, and I am told you have a keen mind and a gift for relating to people. I am convinced that if anyone can put the pieces into a better system (into a single system!), you can.

Are you up to it?

With love,
Your great-great-grandfather,

Reu

ITEM # 3
LETTER FROM SARAI TO GRANDMOTHER LETA

Dear Grandmother,

I know that a girl of seven is not supposed to keep secrets from her mother, but if I write to you, it is almost like sharing with her.

It all started because Papa has several wives. I know that a lot of men have more than one wife, and I know that most of the women talk as if it is a good thing for both men and women, but I don't think that they really mean it. You will probably say that one little snip of a girl is not about to change the way the world looks at things, and maybe I will not, but when I get married, my husband will have to agree that I will be his only wife.

The point is, that Abram and his brothers Nahor and Haran, and his sister Tzilla, and I and my kid brothers Jared and Kenan, not to mention that third woman (whose name you will never catch me pronouncing) and her brats, have grown up acting like one family one day, and like three families the next.

Anyway, Abram started out as if he was doing our father and my mother a great favor by watching me for a few hours. Then he would offer to take me off their hands (at first, so he would not have to tend the camels, I am sure). It gradually reached the point where I could see he enjoyed being with me – but not as much as I am simply thrilled to be with him. We started taking longer and longer walks...

There was the day when we were looking at a bunch of trees and rocks, each one standing for some supposed (please forgive me, but that is how I feel about it!) god, who rules over some part of life in this world. I could not help myself – I am not sure how I put it – but I asked Abram if it does not make more sense to think of only one god who rules over all of this, and over us too. You could have knocked me over with a feather when he looked at me with eyes wide open and said, 'You know, I think you have hit on something.'

Abram no longer objects when Mother asks him to 'take care' of me, and I love it! Grandma, when I grow up I am going to marry that man, and he will agree to have only one wife. I'll bet I can make him wait for me.

Father, Mother, my real brothers, and all my pretend brothers and sisters are all well, almost one happy family.

I hope that you will be able to come and visit with us some day, somehow. I would love to actually meet you.

Your loving granddaughter,

Sarai

ITEM # 4
LETTER FROM LETA TO SARAI

Dear Sarai,

I always wanted a daughter or granddaughter with spunk, but you are more than I ever hoped for.

Your letter was almost a year in getting to me. Who knows how long my letter will take to get to you, but we do the best we can.

Your idea about 'One God' is a really wild one. What would happen if he decided to sleep late? ... or something distracted Him?

Your dream about any man agreeing to limit himself to one wife will probably never come to pass.

And then, of course, your thinking, at your tender young age, that Abram is the one for you might just be another case of your having 'one' on your mind.

But that, at least, is possible. I'll tell you what. I will try to get your grandfather to agree to take the long trek to Ur with some caravan, and to let me go along with him, if we can find a good one headed that way. By then you will be a bit older, Abram and Terah will have had a chance to survey the field of eligible bachelors. And by then, Abram and you will know if you look at things the same way. If it makes sense to me, I will plant the idea with your father and mother, and maybe pull a few strings. I will work on the idea; you work on Abram.

Grandpa and I are well; your uncles, aunts and cousins are in good health. I won't bore you with details, but we have made a good life here.

Your loving grandmother,
Leta

ITEM # 7
AGREEMENT BETWEEN ABRAM AND SARAI
AND THEIR THREE PARENTS

This Covenant of Marriage is entered into this day of the barley-harvest new moon in the twentieth year of King Nimrod, between Tahsha and her son Abram on the one hand, and between Kamullah and her daughter Sarai on the other hand, with Terah, father of both Abram and Sarai, as surety for all parties.

It is agreed that Abram and Sarai are to be married to each other, and that they are to be dowered as befits their status and according to the usage of Ur.

It is agreed that Abram will have no other wife but Sarai as long as Sarai shall live.

It is understood that there are those who cast doubt on whether a marriage of two so closely related can be fruitful, and all parties concerned agree to accept such risk.

Sarai pledges her whole-hearted participation in Abram's vision of One God, and in his resolve to disseminate this vision.

Sarai further agrees to follow Abram to whatever land this vision and resolve may carry him.

If and when blessed with a son, Abram and Sarai understand that he will be charged with the mission of continuing this vision and resolve.

Terah, Tahsha and Kamullah, while not participants in this vision, pledge it their sympathetic support.

ITEM # 9
LETTER FROM SARAI TO SERUG AND WIFE

Dear Great-Grandfather and Great-Grandmother,

It is almost two years since Father, Abram, Lot and I left with a considerable entourage in pursuit of our bold plan to settle in Canaan. It is exactly two years since Grandpa Nahor died.

I never had a clear picture of who felt his loss the most. You lost a son; Great-Grandpa Reu lost a grandson; my Father lost a father to whom he was very closely attached. After all, it isn't everyone who names a son after a living grandfather. I suppose that Grandpa was always in poorer health than anyone (except, perhaps, Father) realized. Abram and I think of him every day.

In any case, Abram and I could see how it hurt Father to walk every day in places his own father used to frequent and not see him, and that by the time a month had passed, he was uncharacteristically urging Abram and me to pull up stakes and head for his (ours as well) long-dreamed-of Canaan. As you very well know, Uncle Nahor cautioned them to go slowly, and Abram, much to my surprise, was the essence of practicality. I am still figuring that man out.

Abram, of course, has never wavered from his dream of locating in an area that will allow his vision of one God-Creator to take root. For some reason he is convinced that Canaan is the one spot on earth where that God can be fully revealed. Call it one more bit of insight that he ascribes to a direct communication from the Most High. I dare say that he will never be completely satisfied until he is there.

To make a long story short, Abram, with the help of Nahor, and as he puts it, with a 'mega-boost from Great-Grandpa Serug and Great-Great-Grandpa Reu,' began tentatively laying the groundwork for a system of caravans to begin to regularize trade along the fertile rim around the great desert. This would carry out a dream that your father planted in his mind years ago. For one thing, it will help to lessen the distance between us. For another, as it lessens the distance for others, our system will grow.

Well, we are not in Canaan; I cannot tell you when we will be. Somewhere along the way, we ran into a group of shepherds from a town called Kharran. Father, for whom the death of Grandfather Nahor opened up the raw wound left by Uncle Haran's death, said, 'It is a sign; we must go there.'

It is truly a lovely place, this town Kharran. It has everything that Father wants, and goes a long way toward fulfilling my requirements.

Abram, to be sure, was ready to push on after the rainy season ended. Father did not budge. Now a second rainy season will shortly be over. Father, more than ever, talks as if he has found a new home.

Abram and I have talked incessantly. He and I have come to the conclusion that at this point we cannot move on and leave Father here. (Our nephew Lot is still an unknown quantity, many good qualities, but unreliable.) Abram, as always, is fascinating. As he puts it, 'The Most High is using this situation to give me a lesson in the importance of family ties and family loyalty.'

As to the final, but most important of concern for Abram and me, the wind blows both ways. I am still not pregnant, and I am already fifty-two years old. You know of all the talk that went around when Grandmother and Mother, may they rest in peace, agreed that we marry – how the 'old wives' kept their tongues wagging, how the healers and midwives were split in their appraisal of our prospects for a fruitful marriage. Maybe the pessimists were right and a half-brother and half-sister should not marry.

Anyway, Abram was and remains the one for me, and Abram has never touched another woman – not even one of my servant girls. So, it is the two of us, forever. Some days, Abram is convinced that God will bless us with children only in Canaan; some days, he has the feeling that we should settle in and make ourselves comfortable here – and hope! I don't know what to think either.

For the foreseeable future, we will stay in Kharran. With every passing month, life gets easier here, lines of communication and commerce come closer to being reliable, and we are beginning to find, from time to time, men and women who are open to the truth of One God. In all honesty both Abram and I, as we talk to people from the four points of the compass, have a continual opportunity to refine our own ideas.

Which leads me to my parting tidbit. Father, who has never lost his interest in making and distributing idols and icons, keeps coming across new materials, new patterns and new techniques from all over the world. At least he is happy!

Please send us, by any means you can, any and all news. We hope that you are all well.

With deepest affection,

Sarai

ITEM # 11
LETTER FROM ABRAM TO NAHOR

Dear Nahor,

First of all, let me reassure you that our father is well. As he keeps on saying, 'It takes more than a bumpy caravan ride to bother Terah.' I had never expected him to take the lead when Sarai and I first seriously discussed leaving Ur for Canaan.

I had, as you well know, a complicated agenda which led me to leave the lovely city of Ur. I can hardly fault you for the mocking tone in which you would say, 'Abram hears these odd voices.' But to me, the voice of the Most High has been eminently real. I appreciate your concession of at least the possibility, which to date I have not convinced you is more than a slim one, that there is but One God, and that He created all that we see above and below and in all four directions. I appreciate your making it clear to me that this truth is nowhere near finding acceptance in the land between the Two Rivers. In any case, the same insight that led me to this truth has led me to see in the concept, current among those along the shores of the great sea, of a Supreme Being (even if they sort of interpret this being as a 'team leader') a step in the right direction. Eventually I hope to move onward to Canaan, but as I will explain, not too soon.

Our father, as we all know, is thoroughly attuned to the idea of many gods, who are best visualized with the help of a physical representation. Obviously, in and around Ur, and in Kharran as well, there are many who share this way of thinking. But I get ahead of myself.

On the other hand, our father has unconventional and advanced views on commerce, and as we both agree, there is a great deal to be said for his ideas on trade. As you know, we had followed the River Perat maybe halfway to Damascus, when the Khabu tributary to the north intrigued him. Nestled in the headwaters was this lovely town of Kharran. Father, in his own inimitable, romantic way, was struck by the similarity to our own dear brother Haran's name. Nothing could dissuade him from wintering here. Of course, it is now the third winter, and I doubt if he will ever leave this veritable paradise.

It was, as you can surmise, easy for me to 'persuade' him to make Kharran the headquarters of an expanded family trade enterprise. He loves the thrill of scouting far and wide to find things of beauty and utility for people, and to find people who can use what he has located. And in contrast to his reluctance to turn a real profit on his lovely idols (as he always says, 'My reward is in knowing that I have connected people with one of the forces that surround us'), he has no objection to being rewarded for his vision and enterprise in the world of trade.

For me, it is time to think about moving on. I have every intention of holding up my end of our expanding enterprise. To you I can confide that, as much as I share Father's and your ambition of financial success, my dream is of opening up a way to reach ever more people with my vision of the One True God. I find that if I set the truth before fifty or a hundred people, that two or three or four will develop an interest and one will change his or her way of thinking. The answer, then, is to talk to thousands and tens of thousands!

For the time being, I cannot leave Father here alone for any length of time. I will probably soon start some traveling. Over time, I hope to make connections in Damascus, in one or two places in Canaan, and in the semi-desert to the south. Eventually, we can reach up to Ugarit and southward to Egypt, and go on to forge bonds with some of the sea-faring communities.

I know that you are not much for traveling, but do get passing caravans to carry word to Father, to our nephew Lot, and to Sarai and me.

Your devoted brother,

Abram

ITEM # 14
LETTER FROM NAHOR TO ABRAM

Dear Abram,

I had been meaning to write to Sarai and to you long before now, but things have been extremely busy.

First, family. Milkah, thanks to the goddess of childbirth (I hope you don't mind my adherence to our grandfather Nahor's and great-grandfather Serug's way of speaking) has given birth to additional children since you left. All is well.

You remember Utz, Buz and especially Kemuel. Buz always has his head sunk into some scroll or other; I think we will send him to the Academy in Ugarit. Utz and Kemuel have developed an interest in commerce; I see them as being managers-in-training. Pildash and Yidlaf, the twins, who were too young for you to really know, are always trying to make things. In any case, all of them have made friends here, and know how to use connections. Within a few years, they will be able to take over whatever we have going here, and be able to expand it.

Betuel, on the other hand, while his mind is open to anything and everything, misses his grandfather terribly. Sooner rather than later, we expect that he will join our father in Kharran, and probably let himself be put to work by his grandfather.

I am not sure what I will do. If we succeed in getting the caravans on any kind of dependable schedule, I may even divide my time between Ur (or rather our Nahor village compound) and Kharran. Don't expect me to follow you to the unsettled area known as Canaan; on the other hand, when Betuel and I move westward you may feel free to move there yourself.

By the way, your letter reached me in about six weeks. We certainly can communicate with each other more frequently than we have been doing. If we build on our contacts at the various oases, we may even be able to provide a means of faster communication, if ever it is needed. Let us both work on it.

Remember me to our half-sister and your wife Sarai. Keep an eye on Father for the both of us.

With brotherly affection,

Nahor

ITEM # 15
LETTER FROM ABRAM TO NAHOR

Dear Nahor,

First of all, a family update: Our Father (may his years increase) is in amazingly good health and spirits. I don't remember the last time that I have seen a repetition of the deep sadness that took hold of him when our late Grandpa Nahor died. On the other hand, there are days when our nephew Lot looks the spitting image of his father, our poor brother Haran, and then Father is all wistfulness. Frankly, I sometimes find it unbelievable that the two of us found the strength to go on, not to mention Father.

Speaking of Lot, when the time comes for Sarai and me to push on, we will take him with us, if only to get him out of Father's hair. He has a generous streak, but he is the soul of impracticality. Sarai and I can usually put a damper on his excess energy when we have to, but Father is not tough enough.

I must report to you on Betuel. I give him high marks in loyalty, honesty, intelligence, imagination and organizational sense. He has proven to be an extremely quick study, and is an ideal complement to our Father. They trust each other, and go out of their way to accommodate each other. By the time that Sarai and I are ready to move on westward, he should be solid enough to be all the family and all the managerial resource that Father needs to have close by.

Sarai, I am happy to say, is in good health and fully attuned to developments here. She has been a wonderful partner in the unfolding vision of the One True God. She is very adept at, and shows great initiative in, taking a critical but sympathetic look at every idea I have. As a result, our understanding and insight are constantly expanding. She has, in a way, adopted the One God project as a substitute for the child she does not yet have.

Sarai, as you will remember her, loves to have people agree with her. The rare tension that we have around here is when she gets over-enthusiastic in her attempt to proselytize our Father. She should know better – and have more respect! – he is her father too. She has a way of taking advantage of the fact that she is her mother's only daughter. But with all that, I am proud of the people that she has won over to our vision.

Together, we have put together an interesting team. We have a small but intense nucleus of people who are true believers. There is a large group who have considerable sympathy, and concede some merit in the idea of One God. There are many who find a great deal to criticize in the variety of religious practices that abound – but are not moved to try any changes. And of course, there are many, many people who are still quite content with things as they are.

I will be the first to admit that on almost every caravan (whether ours or a friend's) that passes this way, I place not only traders, but also kindred, sympathetic spirits who keep their eyes and ears open for expressions of interest in our concept of One True God. They also bring me ideas and teachings that are compatible with my concept of God and which can enhance our impact upon the world. There is no conflict between the two objectives; in a practical sense they can each lend support to the other.

I have been working on a charter of sorts to set up a working relationship between us: an interface between our shared commercial concerns and my own spiritual objectives. I have been working as well on building a cadre of people who can be trusted with key responsibilities, providing them with clear instructions. Now that we almost count on getting word back and forth in close to a month, we can share our ideas more easily. I am confident the day will come when the caravans will be so secure that we will be able to entrust valuables and even people to them.

Please convey my fondest regards to Great-Grandpa Serug and Great-Great-Grandpa Reu and to all the family.

Fondly,
Abram

ITEM # 18
CONTRACT BETWEEN ABRAM AND ELIEZER

Memorandum of Understanding between Abram of Ur and Kharran and Eliezer of Damascus

1. Abram extends to Eliezer an offer of a senior position with Abram, and Eliezer accepts same, on condition that he is tenured in this position.

2. Abram acknowledges the value of contacts and expertise accumulated by Eliezer, and agrees to compensate him accordingly. Eliezer will bring with him originals or copies of any papers, documents and files that he originated.

3. Eliezer takes note of the significance to Abram and Sarai of the belief in the One God/Creator, and will cooperate wholeheartedly with this part of Abram's agenda in whatever ways are necessary. Abram agrees not to press for a public avowal by Eliezer of such a belief.

4. Eliezer will discontinue the use of either of his former names (except as needed to identify himself to his contacts). Abram, in deference to Eliezer's years of acceptance of forms of worship common to these parts, and realizing that these forms of worship are held dear to the close family of both Eliezer and himself, agrees to refer to Eliezer only by such titles as 'household elder.'

5. Eliezer will proceed to engage, on a confidential basis at first, the services of individuals, and to create cooperative agreements with organizations, to advance all the goals of Abram and his family.

6. Abram accepts Eliezer's proposal that Damascus be a temporary center of operations, and that Eliezer will operate out of that location. Abram agrees that for whatever period of time proves to be necessary, discretion is indicated as to Eliezer's role.

7. Abram asserts that within ten or fifteen years, a headquarters location will be set up in Canaan. This headquarters will be strategically located to the major trade routes. Eliezer agrees to relocate with Abram at that time.

ITEM # 22
MEMORANDUM FROM TERAH TO SERUG

Dear Grandpa Serug,

It is now six years since Abram, Sarai, Lot and myself left Ur. In all honesty, my failure to write to you in all this time is hardly due to the difficulty of communication. We all know that, thanks to the efforts of Abram and Nahor, letters do get through most of the time.

As I come back to myself, I marvel at how completely the death of my father Nahor, of blessed memory, paralyzed my emotions. To an outsider, the energetic way I promoted moving out of Ur in the direction of Canaan was proof that I was in control. Actually, it only pointed to my inability to function any longer in Ur, and the difficulty I had in functioning at all. Looking back, I realize that you and Great-Grandpa Reu must have felt that I was totally insensitive to your feelings and needs at the death of a son and grandson.

It has taken me all this time to emerge from my sadness. The only activity I really kept up was my idol-making. I hectored every passing caravan chief into looking for fresh materials, creative designs and new customers, and talked myself into believing that I was actively involved in life. In retrospect, if Abram and Sarai had not brought to me every detail, every problem and every decision of our newly-expanded trade enterprise, I don't know where I would be today. I think they realized all along that I felt they were bothering me. It is to their credit that they never let on – or let up!

In any case, I think that I am now back to myself, mostly. So let me convey to you, as I see it, the bad news and the good.

First, Abram and Sarai still have no children. It is not for want of searching for advice or assistance. It is probably a failure that feeds on itself. At the moment, I am encouraging them to relax and enjoy life here in Kharran. Abram and Sarai are convinced that only through their children will the belief in One God be able to continue and to grow. I once made the mistake of suggesting to Abram that he take a second wife. Believe me, that will not happen again.

Second, my grandson Lot is still a mystery. He is such a blend of qualities and shortcomings. His wife is the most curious person I have ever met, and I can never anticipate what they will do next! As much as I would love to have Abram and Sarai stay on here indefinitely, if the price of getting Lot out of here is to have them move away with him, I would say farewell tomorrow.

Third, as much as this old idol-maker cannot go along with the thought of the world having only one god (and an invisible one at that!), it does my heart good to see Abram and Sarai mingling with all sorts of folk, from wherever they come, and talking up the idea (incomprehensible to me) of One Supreme Being who is the creative force behind every thing and every event in this world. One part of me almost wants to cheer when they lose me a customer. Their philosophy must strike a responsive chord in the minds and hearts of many people.

But on the fourth matter, we can all agree. Our little trading enterprise is no longer little. Nahor, I trust, has given you reports on what we (to be honest, mostly Abram) are accomplishing. We now know by name (and are known by) people at dozens of oases, the chiefs of scores of caravans, and tradesmen and merchants too numerous to count. Abram has established all sorts of contacts, and has enlisted the services of a few key people.

A few examples will illustrate what I mean. He made contact with a fascinating person in Damascus, whom he refers to only as 'my old man' (I think he gave him the code name of Eliezer). He has joined our enterprise –

lock, stock and barrel. He has brought with him a fantastically complete file about people and places in every area I ever heard of. He even told me things about Ur and some of its people that I did not know. He has a tremendous purchasing file which details what can be bought where, and at what price. He has a small but impressive file of individuals who can be called on for what he calls 'security operations.' Abram has enlisted the help of many others, but I think his 'old man' will rise to the top.

On the other hand, Abram, as you can surmise, has never lost sight of his goal, which not so long ago was my goal as well, to settle in the land of Canaan. Practical person that he is, he has begun to do two things. One, he is grooming Betuel to take over here. For me, Betuel is a balanced combination of family, friend and partner; no complaints there. And two, he is making all kinds of little moves that are designed to set up a kind of operational headquarters somewhere in the south of Canaan.

He has come to some sort of understanding with a trio operating in the south of Canaan named Aner, Eshkol and Mamre. I have not met them, but I am impressed with what I hear. I hope he knows what he is doing.

At the same time, he has begun to delegate all kinds of functions, so that he can have more time for what I would describe as things of the spirit. I, for one, have no cause to question his judgment. Time will tell.

This has been a long letter, and it has tired me. Please get together a report of events in Ur and send it to me. The chances are that I will not be traveling to Ur, Canaan, or anywhere else. I have it good here.

Your loving grandson,

Terah

ITEM # 24
LETTER FROM TERAH TO ABRAM

Dear Abram,

I am impressed with what you have found in Canaan. The picture that we have had of a wild, untamed 'land of the West' obviously does not match reality.

I am even more impressed by the way in which you have made things develop. I must say that my boys have done me proud. Nahor, back in Ur, is a credit to the name he bears. You, in spite of your obsession with propagating this idea of a one-and-only 'Most High,' have been the one to prove the validity of my theories of basing trade on human relations.

Just remember, Abram, not to let your 'One God' visions keep you from maintaining friendly, not to say mutually beneficial, relations with Hittites, Canaanites, Philistines or whomever. At the risk of being repetitious, let me remind you that your father is the best idol-maker in this part of the world, and that almost everyone in our family treasures his products.

Again I remind you that the cycle of wet and dry years is more severe in your new home. Try to set up a fallback plan, and feel free to check it out with me.

Give my best to Sarai, and to Lot as well.

With fatherly affection,

Terah

ITEM # 27
EXTRACT FROM CORPORATE FILES OF THE
UR-KHARRAN-HEBRON TRADING COMPANY

Standing Instructions To All Employees of Ur-Kharran-Hebron Trading Company

(1) Know when to maintain a low profile. Always present the image of a normal business enterprise.

(2) Notwithstanding the need to operate at a profit:

(a) Never neglect any opportunity to protect the life and interest of family members.

(b) Always have transport available for whatever purpose may arise.

(c) Keep operational headquarters directly informed of all developments. If in doubt – communicate.

(d) Use discretion as to what information to reveal to individuals we are interested in, and when. When uncertain as to how to proceed, consult headquarters. Ask yourself, 'What would Abram have wanted?'

(3) Keep in mind Abram's message of One God, and the priority of his mission of disseminating this message.

(4) Retain in positions of trust only those with a bona fide loyalty to the Covenant of Abram.

(5) Share these instructions only with those with a 'need to know.' Clear everything with headquarters.

ITEM # 29
ABSTRACT OF DOCUMENT

A reference to a highly classified document, alluding to success in identifying individuals who can map out the maze of political and hierarchical connections in Egypt while pinpointing avenues of communication and possible commonality of interest.

FOR DETAILS,
REFER TO FILE "BET-SHIN 18"

ITEM # 32
LETTER FROM ELIEZER TO RA'AMA

Dear Ra'ama,

I hope that all is well with you and our brethren in Damascus. On the basis of reports I receive, it seems that you do not really miss your cousin Eliezer. (I would prefer not to put into writing the explanation of this name – which contains the name of a different sort of god – and how I come to be using it.)

It takes a long time for information to get from one place to another, but if there is one thing that I learned during my years in Damascus, it is how to sort out what is reliable. The point is, that the archival material and procedural protocols that I provided for Havila and that whole crew left them quite able to carry on after I left, so I have a clear conscience about leaving to follow Abram's star. Your cousin is an honorable man.

Eighteen years after leaving Damascus, I am now absolutely certain that I made a wise choice. First of all, Abram is an inspired man of vision, and Sarai is an ideal partner in all he has undertaken. Having been associated with them ever since that fateful day when I took over the caravan to Kharran at the last moment, I could never return to an environment which thinks in terms of a whole gamut of divine powers. Spiritual matters aside, I can assert with assurance that I have never met anyone who can hold a candle to Abram. He never misses an opportunity to give his grandfather Nahor credit for creating a most ambitious trading network, and to his father Terah for fleshing out the details. The fact is, he took over what was really a rather rudimentary concept (as I appreciate now!), and used it as a foundation to build up a very sophisticated, efficient and far-sighted organization. All of us have benefitted from his genius.

Let me give you one small example of this leadership quality. When I arrived, I brought with me a small group of military types, to help Abram be prepared for all sorts of eventualities. One can never know what might happen. Canaan consists of small islands of civilization surrounded by a sea of restless people. Abram used my seventy-two people to beef up a motley band of about two hundred and thirty, loyal to three local dukes (make a notation of the names: Aner, Eshkol and Mamre), enlisted a small crew of extremely competent scouts, located two weapons wizards, a master strategist and a gifted tactician, and has integrated these three hundred and eighteen individuals into a top-notch militia force.

As you know, Abram has no children, and is beginning to despair of ever being blessed with offspring. I would do anything within my power to help this wonderful couple realize their dream, but facts are facts, and I might as well be realistic. As things stand now, I am in as good a position as anyone to be the son they do not have. Furthermore, I am with Abram every day. No one knows more about Abram's business than I do. So, if a choice of a successor were to be made today, I might very well be next in line to inherit from him. I must admit that this thought appeals to me, perhaps more than it should.

Of course, you will breathe none of this to anyone.

Your cousin,

Eliezer

ITEM # 35
FILE ENTRY

A letter from a seafaring trader, based in Tyre

To: Our friend and colleague, Abram

We have inquired of those who study the utterances of our priests and of those who serve Ba'al and other local deities. Those in whom wisdom abides share the view that the rainless conditions of the past two years will be repeated for one or two more years, following which the cycle will return to a period of the normal, more generous, rainfall.

We look forward to continued close cooperation, and to sharing in whatever benefits you are able to derive from putting our advice to you to good use.

If you are ever presented with the opportunity of referring to us individuals of established integrity, we should be happy to interview them.

Your faithful and appreciative friend,

Yokshan

ITEM # 38
FILE ENTRY

A reference to and summary of a classified document:

It is common knowledge that the Pharaoh asserts as a royal prerogative the right to conscript any woman into his harem. We have reliable evidence that in the case of a married woman, charges of a capital crime are lodged against her husband, who is then summarily executed.

FOR DETAILS
REFER TO FILE "BET-SHIN 28"

ITEM # 39
FILE ENTRY

Document Summary

(extremely sensitive document / Source withheld)

Pharaoh, according to a source within his harem, has predictable likes and dislikes in women.

Those who do not pass the final screening are ousted from the palace with three days' rations.

Many, though still virgins, have difficulty returning to their former status. Some, on the other hand, have capitalized on their experience, claiming that their value has risen.

(It is clear that details which might identify the source of this information have been withheld.)

FOR DETAILS
THOSE WITH CLEARANCE
REFER TO FILE "SHIN-SHIN 09"

ITEM # 40
FILE ENTRY

Document Summary

Record of expenditures for the purchase of three houses and three fields in the vicinity of Ur of the Chaldees.

Records, with receipts properly attached, following the transfer to three individuals 'in appreciation of services rendered.'

Justification entry clarifies the connection to information referred to in the previous two items.

ITEM # 42
LETTER FROM ABRAM
TO PHOTUM-RE IN EGYPT

Noble Sir,

Your Excellency knows all that occurs in the Royal Court, and is acquainted with the royal family and other nobility and their families. I have long been impressed with the wisdom and commercial acumen of the first families of Egypt, and the grace and intelligence of their women is legend.

Should circumstances ever arise that allow me an extended absence from the Hebron area, I hope to visit my brothers in Egypt. It is my desire to meet with individuals with experience in spices and precious stones, and it is not impossible that we might cement such an alliance by taking into our household a princess from one such family, who would occupy a post of trust and honor, in keeping with her lineage.

We look forward to meeting you in person.

In sincerest friendship,

Abram

ITEM # 43
FILE ENTRY

Memorandum

From: Yokshan
To: Abram

Time is short. It is now possible to predict with certainty that the drought conditions will continue for a third consecutive year, creating significant cumulative drought damage.

Forewarned is forearmed. Do what you can to protect your interests. We rely on your goodwill and generosity to protect ours.

ITEM # 44
FILE ENTRY

**** Sensitive ****

(Need to know only)

From: Inventory Control

To: Accounting
Administrative Headquarters

(1) A twelve-camel caravan, laden with grain, has been dispatched to Yokshan.

(2) Charge to accounts as follows:

(a) Drought damage control: 40%

(b) Operation Nile Valley: 60%

(3) Pursuant to instructions of Eliezer, care was taken to list this as a shipment of wine and sheep's wool.

ITEM # 45
ABRAM'S JOURNAL

Sarai and I are agreed that it makes eminent good sense for us to weather out the coming drought in Egypt. The potential long-term advantages, when added to the precarious nature of life under drought conditions in the always arid Negev, outweigh the risks of life in Egypt. Sarai is satisfied that she can be sufficiently well fortified with information on the ins and outs of what it takes to please – and, more to the point, to displease! – the great Pharaoh, if it comes to that.

We both understand, and are prepared to accept, the risk that the one or more daughters of noble families who might possibly join our entourage will assume that the arrangement is a matrimonial one. Between us, once we have returned home, we will be able to make it clear to everyone that this is not the case. If the new commercial undertakings go as well as we predict, the prosperity that will accrue to the Egyptian partner, and the fact that we can maintain his sister or daughter in the lap of luxury, will serve to take the edge off any potential disappointment.

ITEM # 46
LETTER FROM ABRAM TO TERAH

Dear Father,

I have written to you a number of times of my economic interest in Egypt. In many ways, they are ahead of anything we do here in Canaan, and, for that matter, in the Land of the Two Rivers. I keep turning over in my head all sorts of models that might help create a trading organization to connect Ur, Kharran, Damascus, northern and southern Canaan, the Philistine territories and Egypt. The fact is, there are no two points which have not at some time or another been linked by an occasional caravan or sporadic travel and trade. But you were correct from the beginning: there is much to be gained by creating a system of regular, interconnected caravan routes.

I have decided we must go one step further: we must set up person-to-person links. Sarai and I will be embarking on a risky venture to put an Egyptian connection into operation.

As you have been reading in the periodic reports that I have had sent to you, and as you correctly anticipated, the past three years have been very dry. There are those who have developed a method of storing water over an extended period, but, to no one's surprise, they are reluctant to share this information. Most people just go where the water is.

Sarai and I could conceivably make do with what we have for one more year, bringing in food supplies and other necessities, and using what little water there is here for non-food-growing needs, but we have decided not to do so. For one thing, it is just as well that neighbors roundabout do not know everything about our capabilities, and, more to the point, when droves of people are making their way to Egypt, we have a tailor-made opportunity to scout out the land of the Nile without being too conspicuous.

There are risks and opportunities. I need hardly tell you that travel is dangerous. By now, we have friends in many places, but friends can do only so much. One serious hazard is that the Pharaoh's 'beauty scouts' send him reports on every good-looking woman they hear of. An invitation to 'apply for' a spot in the Pharaoh's harem is not to be turned down. My information is that almost routinely, if the woman is married, her husband is accused of some trumped-up charge and, as likely as not, will be executed. Fortunately, we can truthfully tag Sarai as my sister. It should help. More to the point, we have been successful in getting hold of information which I consider extremely reliable as to what displeases the king. Sarai is practicing – and she can with little difficulty manage – not to pass muster. We will quite happily survive the 'dishonor' of her being rejected.

The opportunity to create economic growth remains high. The main point is to forge a few person-to-person bonds to facilitate extending our regular trade operations into Egypt. The Nile Valley provides an extremely wide variety of products for which we can pinpoint a need and a market. The people there know a good bit about breeding, training and using camels, and I might be able to hire one or two good men. They have contacts all along the coastal route. Their information about routes through the Sinai desert and the Negev area, not to mention essential details about oases, can be found nowhere else. In addition (you know my wife!) we can probably find a competent housekeeper for Sarai. My own thought would be to recruit a woman from the family of one of my new commercial contacts.

Finally, and, to be completely aboveboard with you, I am driven to investigate reports I have received about individuals and small groups whose ideas are compatible with my concept of One God. (The name Ikhnaton keeps surfacing.) It is good to build bridges and compare notes. And, truth to tell, such people can be called on, hopefully, in an hour of need.

Time will tell. I will quite possibly not be writing until we return to Canaan. If I can devise a way of getting some kind of communication through Mamre, he should be able to keep you posted as to how we are faring. In the meantime, remember us to Great-Grandpa Serug.

Your loving son,

Abram

ITEM # 47
ABRAM'S JOURNAL

Medical Evaluation Report

From: Gezer Healing Center
To: Abram

We regret to inform you that we can arrive at no clear explanation for the inability of Sarai to conceive. We have investigated many possible explanations for this misfortune, but are as yet unable to establish any cause for her barrenness.

It is, of course, just possible that the extremely unsettling conditions with which your household has had to contend throughout your married years has taken its toll of both of you. Unfortunately, we can neither make any concrete recommendation or venture a definitive opinion as to the permanence of her problem.

ITEM # 50
FILE ENTRY

** Confidential **

From: **Photum-Re,** Deputy Administrator, Royal Residence

To: **Abram**

To our friend and benefactor, Abram.

The woman called Sarai, the one identified as your sister, is in good health. Despite our constant advice, she gives no promise of advancing to the inner circle from which the Pharaoh chooses his consorts. If I did not know better, I would say that she is not trying hard enough to please.

We advise you to be prepared to reassume responsibility for her care. We extend our sympathy for your disappointment.

We are sharing this information with our cousin Locum-Re. He and his daughter Hagar will continue to do all they can to make your stay, and possibly that of the woman Sarai, pleasant and profitable.

We thank you for the gift of delectable fruit from the lands of the Tigris.

ITEM # 52
FILE ENTRY

Memorandum

From: Locum-Re

To: Abram

The woman Sarai, who we are told is your sister, has been precipitously ousted from the women's residence in the Pharaoh's compound. It is not for us to judge how great a loss this is for your family.

For the moment, it is wise to have her stay in our household. Our youngest daughter Hagar, who has not much to do, can see to her needs. Indeed, if Sarai will have her, we are willing to have her in time join your illustrious household. She can, in addition to taking responsibility for whatever Sarai needs, provide you and our fledgling trading enterprise with valuable information about our Egyptian customs, and perhaps even do a bit of translating.

ITEM # 53
LETTER FROM AMEN-PHERA, *Secretary To The Great And Divine Pharaoh*
TO ABRAM

Dear Abram,

Strange things have been happening. The woman Sarai, whom Your Excellency refers to as your sister, is described by normally reliable sources as your wife. The Royal Court understandably takes a dim view of deceptive statements made by 'guests' of our kingdom. Fortunately, as events unfolded, the Pharaoh was protected from any act which might evoke the displeasure of the divine powers; but many in the Royal Court are critical of your words and actions.

It is your good fortune that a number of our first citizens have come forward to vouch for you. These include, as you know, prime movers in the innovative new system of trade which brings to us spices and other items necessary to our civilized life, in return for those good things produced by the genius of our Egyptian economy. I myself have been moved by the confidence placed in you by our dear and valued friend Locum-Re. His judgment and the obvious confidence he has placed in you by allowing the Princess Hagar to join you have swayed even his Great and Divine Majesty.

We look forward to significant benefits to the Royal Court and to its individual members (not the least of whom is your reliable servant), as well as to our beloved land of Egypt. We are ready, for our part, to assist in making this undertaking prosper.

In its growth will we all find peace and good fortune.

Respectfully yours,

Amen-Phera

ITEM # 54
LETTER FROM ABRAM TO NAHOR

Dear Nahor,

Well, we pulled it off! For a while there, Sarai and I were in quite a lot of danger. But, with God's help, we emerged unscathed.

The point is, we now have a knowledgeable and trusted friend in high places. He will provide advice and behind-the-scenes assistance as we put to work all I have learned during our winter in Egypt.

We will in short order have an office in Zoan which will serve as the southwest anchor for our growing enterprise. If you ever receive a direct communication from Locum-Re, honor it as if I had sent it.

Locum-Re has made a suggestion. He took one look at the map of the territory we serve, and seeing the four rivers that transverse it, the Hideckel, the Euphrates, the Jordan and the Nile, suggested that we call our enterprise the Four Rivers Trading Company. It has a good sound to me. Tell me what you think. Run it by Father as well.

Sarai and I have agreed to another suggestion. Locum-Re has a daughter Hagar, who was at loose ends at home, and for some reason not interested in marriage. He asked us, really Sarai, to take her on as a handmaiden; she really has a lot of talents. Hagar (everyone here calls her 'the Egyptian') is now part of our household; I hope it works out.

We will now be having monthly reports, emanating from an Administrative Headquarters. We will have more and more routine items to pass on. Just send everything, even the trivial, on to them, also on a monthly basis. This should contribute to a smoother operation.

Sarai sends her best. She looks truly well. Tell Father I will write soon, and explain the new, more formal, setup that expansion requires.

What do you hear from Ur? We must work on ways to have caravans and other contacts operate more frequently and with greater regularity.

Your loving brother,

Abram

ITEM # 57
FILE ITEM

Four Rivers Trading Company

Annual Report

As the attached exhibits and accounts show, our first year of full operations has justified both the efforts and resources we have expended and the confidence placed in this novel idea. With one stroke, albeit not as simple as it appears on the surface, we have put into place:

(1) a reliable source of supply for an unbelievable variety of items needed in all this vast territory
(2) a stable market for products for which there had not previously been a sufficient outlet
(3) a close-knit operating team which can provide reliable information and support for all our friends, and
(4) an unprecedented capacity to communicate Abram's vision of a single Most High One in heaven and on earth, with all the implications of that vision

There is now enhanced interchange among such far-flung places as Zoan in Egypt, Midian, Aram, Kharran, Sumer, Ur and Hebron. In time, with the hoped-for success of the newly opened market with the seafaring folk in Gerar, the far reaches of the Great Sea will be added to our network.

We call upon the directors to increase our budget as befits the scope of our concept and our operations.

ITEM # 59
ABRAM'S JOURNAL

Now that I have been in Canaan for six full years, I am more than ever torn by conflicting emotions.

First, Sarai and I are gratified to find an encouraging level of response to our message of the true and only Most High, Creator of heaven and earth. In spite of the prevalence of pagan ideas and customs, and even their exaggerated manifestation in such places as Sodom, we find almost everywhere five, ten, sometimes even twenty people sensitive to righteousness and spiritual truth. This is much better than the situation in Ur or Kharran.

Second, the concept of unity among diverse peoples has borne fruit in our trading enterprise. This will not only provide funds to enable us to live in comfort, and to finance our efforts to reach out to those who hunger for a word of truth; it will serve as a channel for us to reach others and to allow them to seek us out.

If only I had a son! Sarai is not getting younger – nor am I. Everything that I have created needs to be perpetuated, otherwise our success will seem hollow to me. Eliezer is a fine, capable, dedicated man of integrity. I could ask for no better lieutenant. He has accepted many parts of our vision. But he is not our son, nor is he the unwavering bearer we need to continue our work into the next generation.

ITEM # 60
ABRAM'S JOURNAL

A most remarkable vision! It left me shaking, and I shake still, thirty-six hours later.

The Most High appeared before me. 'Not only will you have a child,' He said, 'you will be the progenitor of an entire nation. Your offspring will spread out: west, east, north, south. This spot of land, in which My unity and your dedication have taken root and borne fruit, will always be yours.'

As the vision melted away into a pillar of fire blended with a heavy pall of black smoke, I felt the Divine Presence as never before. I am more convinced than ever that His word will reach far and wide, especially now that we see the beginning of success in our goal of transmitting the Divine Message across great distances.

ITEM # 63
FILE ENTRY

Memorandum

From: Yokshan

To: Abram

Things go well. I admit that I was a bit skeptical about your commercial plans, but we have exceeded even your most optimistic predictions. I am impressed especially at the new ease and reliability of communications.

I am not as convinced by your talk of a Most High Power, but I do now and then run into individuals who seem open to such a thought. I suppose that your idea does manifest a sort of logic.

May I add that the man Eliezer is unbelievable. He is everywhere, and much of your success is due to him. He promotes the Four Rivers Trading Company almost as if it were his own.

ITEM # 66
LETTER FROM HADORAM TO ABRAM

Dear Cousin Abram,

I must concede that you were right on all counts. Canaan seems to be much more civilized than we all thought it was, and you have quite clearly found a rather settled life. Your commercial ventures, I gather, are quite successful, and we thank you for adding to our prosperity. Even your extreme idea of One God, who actually created the universe, seems to have attracted believers. Some day you will have to tell us more.

The womenfolk here in Ur chide me for not asking for news of children and grandchildren. For our part, the family here is doing well, and growing. From all reports reaching us here, as hopefully from those reaching you as well, Terah and the rest of the Kharran branch of the family are likewise in good health and content.

By the way, please send the man Eliezer this way more often. Everyone is pleased to have dealings with him.

With cousinly greetings,

Hadoram

ITEM # 69
LETTER FROM LOCUM-RE TO ABRAM

Dear Abram,

Greetings to our brother in Canaan. Thank you for the news of our daughter Hagar. You have justified our trust in your judgment in every way. Personally and financially we have done very well. I think that your decision to allow the Pharaoh to go on thinking that all this activity is my doing has been mutually beneficial. Our success enhances the Pharaoh's renown and brings benefits to the incomparable Land of the Nile.

We have introduced your man, the Damascene called Eliezer, to Amen-Phera, secretary to the Pharaoh. How did you find such a jewel?

We are told that you have no children. Have you considered the possibility of bringing Hagar into your personal household? She comes from a line of most fertile women, and she would please you in all ways.

With fraternal greetings,

Locum-Re

ITEM # 73
LETTER FROM ELIEZER TO RA'AMA

Dear Ra'ama,

I did not want to write to you about Lot and my evaluation of him before now because I was not quite sure I could trust myself to be objective. You realize as well as I do what he could have meant for my hopes of some day being the senior partner of all I survey.

Abram and Sarai still have no son. This means that there is no natural line of succession to the leadership of the Four Rivers Trading Company and to Abram's spiritual stake in the vision of the One God. This leaves me very much in the running to take over the Four Rivers operation some day. Until recent events began to unfold, the succession to Abram's property and vision seemed to be spiraling toward Lot, Abram's heir-apparent. But now, things have occurred which suggest that I may yet become the proud owner of at least the Four Rivers operation.

An alliance of four local kings (as they call themselves) overwhelmed a group of five city rulers, including that of Sodom, where Lot has made his home. Abram received a report that Lot was among the prisoners, and in a matter of days mobilized all of his force of three hundred and eighteen of which I wrote to you. It goes without saying that our forces prevailed. There was a victory celebration, with a full-dress thanksgiving service, but Lot was nowhere to be seen. He went right back to that God-forsaken city, Sodom! Abram was crestfallen.

By the way, the lead in the thanksgiving proceedings was taken over by Malki-Zedek, king of the independent city, Shalem. I will have to keep my eyes on the man and on the city.

Abram has the ability to bounce back. But it is clear to me, even though he will not eliminate his support of Lot and his family, that he now realizes that the line of succession cannot be curved in that direction.

All this, I don't have to tell you, puts me on the inside track. Only time will tell.

Otherwise, all is well. Abram's dream and vision are beginning to take root here. I have actually heard Abram referred to as 'God's Prince.' The trading venture is succeeding beyond anyone's wildest dreams, and my position in it is solid.

Do me one favor. Try to pick up any reports coming out of Kharran (you will not be able to get much out of Ur) as to the involvement of Nahor and his family in this or that trading enterprise. Information has come my way to the effect that they are concentrating their energies on sheep-ranching and gradually de-emphasizing their role in the trading operation. They don't seem to have much interest in agriculture. Check this out, please; it would not hurt to be certain.

I close by sending you my wish that whatever god has any power in Damascus may extend to you his or her blessing,

Your ever-loving cousin,

Eliezer

ENTRY # 76
SARAI'S PERSONAL JOURNAL

I wish I knew the cause of our childlessness. Abram and I have gone everywhere, spoken to anyone who claims to know something about the subject, imported exotic herbs from the farthest reaches, but to no avail.

The 'fault' may indeed be mine. It pains me to see Abram look jealously at the youngest of his slaves, and at people he sees wherever he goes, playing happily with children. It pains me even more to realize that others in his situation would have long since taken a second or third wife. He too would have done so, were it not for the pledge that he made to me at the time of our betrothal to the effect that I would be his only wife. I can't help wondering whether he has had second thoughts about that pledge.

I even wonder whether he has begun thinking of my personal maid, Hagar; I have. In any event, it is with a heavy heart that I have decided to propose to him the expedient of having a child by her. I am not sure whether I want him to say yes or no.

ENTRY # 78
ABRAM'S JOURNAL

Summary of
Memorandum of Understanding
among
MYSELF, SARAI and HAGAR

Hagar's New Status

1. Hagar accepts as unequivocal her continued status as Sarai's handmaiden.

2. Sarai approves of sexual relations between Hagar and Abram, with the express purpose of providing an heir to Abram.

3. Abram, Sarai and Hagar are all agreed that Abram has only one wife – Sarai.

4. Hagar and Abram agree that sexual relations will come to an end if and when Hagar produces a male child.

5. Abram agrees to designate such male child as his heir.

6. Abram and Sarai undertake to rear male or female children of Hagar, and to provide for them in a fitting manner.

ENTRY # 81
INTERNAL MEMO

** Confidential **

From: Eli Hazo, Manager, Four Rivers Trading Company
To: Senior Personnel

Trouble brewing! The three-way agreement between Abram, Sarai and Hagar seems to have broken down, now that Hagar is pregnant. Sarai, a very resourceful woman, is subtly making Hagar's life unbearable. I sense an explosion coming, soon.

Eli Hazo

ITEM # 82
FILE ENTRY

Statement of Eligibility

From: Eli Hazo, Manager, Four Rivers Trading Company
To: All employees

Be advised that the woman known as Hagar the Egyptian is entitled to full benefits, protection and courtesy as a member of the extended founding family. However, she is not authorized access to files, and is entitled to information only at the Class Three level.

Eli Hazo

ITEM # 84
FIELD ITEM

Field Report

From: Negev Station # 3
To: Hebron Headquarters
Copy To: Administrative Headquarters

Caught sight of a pregnant woman, obviously quite distraught, wandering aimlessly. Before we could make contact, she was approached by a man of unearthly appearance, who fortunately succeeded in calming her down.

When we finally intercepted her, still a bit confused and rather excited, she immediately asked: 'Do you know how I can get to Hebron?'

With little difficulty we identified her as Hagar the Egyptian, about whom you have previously communicated with us.

We entrusted her to the capable hands of the scout unit of caravan #22-7-18, headed for the lower Sinai. (Details on other necessary shuffling will appear on our regular monthly report.)

They are on their way to Hebron now. We rely on Ophir to ease her return to the household of Abram.

ITEM # 85
FILE ENTRY

Subject: **Letter of Commendation**
From: Administrative Headquarters
To: Staff of Negev Station #3

Well done! We have shared your report with Abram himself. He is very well pleased, and desires that you be heartily commended.

Try to find out more about the person who befriended Hagar. Abram sees in his appearance the hand of the Most High. Confidentially, this entire episode has strengthened his faith and uplifted his morale. You may be proud of your handling of it.

ITEM # 86
FILE ENTRY

General Order

From: Administrative Headquarters
To: All Staff

The enclosed letter of eligibility issued by Eli Hazo is hereby confirmed and given the status of a General Order. All available resources are to be used for the benefit of Hagar and anyone accompanying her.

ITEM # 88
FILE ENTRY

Letter of Eligibility

From: Administrative Headquarters
To: All Stations

Abram has a son named Ishmael. Abram directs that his son be entitled to the full benefit of any and all resources at your command.

It is anticipated that Ishmael will, in due course, be a full partner in the Four Rivers Trading Company and its various allied enterprises.

ITEM # 89
LETTER FROM ELIEZER TO RA'AMA

Dear Ra'ama,

To put it mildly, this has been a most interesting year! It all began when Sarai, the most amazing woman I have ever met, came to a very painful decision. She proposed to Abram (as far as I can judge, on her own initiative) that he endeavor to have a child by the Egyptian servant-woman, Hagar. In a sense, she was freeing Abram, to this limited degree (fated to be not so limited), from a pledge that was made over fifty years ago, that he would never have a second wife. It is a pledge that he made most willingly, and one that he has honored scrupulously.

A man like Abram does not lightly undo a pledge, especially one freely made. He spoke to every sage, near and far, whose judgment and discretion he felt he could trust. In the end, he agreed that the goal of having an heir to carry on, and the fact that this was an implied assumption when he took the original oath, plus Sarai's insistence, justified suspending the oath.

Hagar must be quite a fertile woman. In no time, she was pregnant. Mission accomplished, no? You be the judge.

The formerly docile, cooperative maid began to show flashes of arrogance. I cannot really blame either woman for what happened. Hagar, by her bearing and her attitude, was saying that if she were to be the mother of Abram's heir, her employment contract would have to be replaced with an agreement of a far different sort. Not for me to say that she was wrong!

Sarai, quite naturally, saw things from a completely opposite perspective. Regardless of what some people attribute to me, I cannot read minds, but it seems to me that she looked at Hagar as a kind of surrogate for herself. Only a woman who has waited for a child for over fifty years could really understand what she was feeling. In any event, she leaned on Hagar, as if to make the point that Hagar was still – and forever will be – Sarai's handmaiden.

At one point, Hagar actually ran off; I doubt whether she thought far enough ahead to think through just where she was going. She quickly came back, and friend Abram did a superb job of conflict resolution. The two women will never again be friends (if they ever were), but Abram, once again showing his genius at working with people and with their personalities and needs, got them to call off the fireworks. The balance of Hagar's pregnancy was uneventful, and a couple of months ago, a son, Ishmael, was born.

The dynamic among the two women, the child and Abram changes from day to day. Truth to tell, every change impacts on me. Officially, Ishmael is now Abram's heir (most days, even Sarai agrees) which means that I will never be. I have to admit to myself that it was never meant to be. It was a nice dream while it lasted! My role in the household has been subtly changed, but on the other hand there are now more matters for which Abram relies on me. There are duties for which he trusts no one else, and as the family grows, so does my attachment to Abram, and all that is his.

Still, sometimes I ask, 'What if?'

Your loving cousin,

Eliezer

ITEM # 102
ABRAM'S PERSONAL FILE

Evaluation Report

From: Tekoa Educational Center
To: Abram

Our team has done a thorough evaluation of your son Ishmael. As compared to the level of an average six-year-old, we rate him as follows:

Mathematical reasoning:	*Above average*
Problem solving:	*Average*
Conceptual analysis:	*Slightly above average*
Right and wrong:	*Above average*
Nature skills:	*Just barely acceptable*

We recommend at this time concentration on his strong points.

ITEM # 110
ABRAM'S PERSONAL FILE

Progress Report

From: Tekoa Educational Center
To: Abram

Your son Ishmael, under the tutelage of our competent staff, continues to make solid progress. Compared to the level of an average nine-year old, we rate him:

Mathematical reasoning:	*Superior*
Problem solving:	*Average*
Conceptual analysis:	*Above average*
Right and wrong:	*Satisfactory*
Nature skills:	*Marginally Acceptable*

We recommend the following:

(1) Continued stress on mathematical reasoning and conceptual analysis;

(2) Increased emphasis on nature studies, acquaintance with desert lore and travel/transportation-related skills;

(3) Indoctrination in the lore of the Most High to remain in your hands; begin to apply it to concepts of Right and Wrong.

ITEM # 118
FILE ENTRY

Information Bulletin

From: Administrative Headquarters
To: Senior Personnel

Abram's name has been changed. From now on, he is to be called Abraham. Sarai's name has been changed to Sarah.

These changes are in connection with the continuous process of fine-tuning the overriding concern of Abraham to grow in knowledge of the Most High, Creator of heaven and earth, and to disseminate knowledge of Him in these lands and ultimately far and wide.

You are well advised to reacquaint yourselves with the implications of this belief in the One God.

ITEM # 119
FILE ENTRY
BULLETIN

** Confidential **

From: Eliezer
To: All Key Staff

There is reason to believe that as a parallel development to the assumption by the founding couple of the new names of Abraham and Sarah, by which names they are now exclusively to be known, and to the new emphases which these changes imply, there will at long last be a child born to our founders.

It seems natural to assume that if it be a son, he will be in line to be a full partner, quite possibly the principal partner, in all of Abraham's endeavors. (If it be a daughter, it is our assumption that nothing will change.)

Be advised, in any case, that Abraham has not directed, and indeed may not direct, any change in the status of Ishmael.

Ishmael continues to have access to any information up to and including Class 2 status, and continues to be entitled to full support and unrestricted benefit of all your resources.

ITEM # 120
LETTER FROM ELIEZER TO RA'AMA

Dear Ra'ama,

As I have mentioned to you before, when Abraham needs to confide in someone, he tends to turn to me. Let me go back a step or two. The former Abram experienced one of his rare visions, and the upshot of it was that his name is now changed to Abraham, and Sarai's name is now Sarah. As close as I can tell, the new names are symbolic of a reaffirmation of the pledge made by the One God to Abraham, and, if that is possible, a strengthening of the covenant with this fantastic couple: He and Sarah will found a mighty nation; it will, in the course of time, embody Abraham's dream of disseminating throughout the world the truth of the Most High, who is Creator of the universe, Master of human destiny, supreme Arbiter of justice and ultimate Source of truth. It is, of course, quite an ambitious dream, even as dreams go, but who are we to judge what is possible for such unusual human beings.

If I understand Abraham's words correctly, the vision was directed to him and to Sarah. Abraham the dreamer is also Abraham the practical; and Abraham, husband of Sarah, is also Abraham, father of Ishmael. Which means that his first reaction, as one who has God's ear, was to argue for the existing line of succession, through Ishmael. I have, to be sure, already put into words my firm conviction that there will not soon (if ever) be a second Abraham, with all his many qualities and strengths. There is no question that Ishmael has many strengths, but he also has not a few weak points. He will certainly never be the match of Abraham. The essence of the vision, as transmitted to me by Abraham, is that the One God has told him that Sarah will bear a son (at the age of 90!) who will, in time, carry on the mission and the dream, and that Ishmael will somehow be the founder of a mighty nation. Well, it's a big world!

So, prepare for another thoroughgoing reorganization within the Abraham household. I just hope that nothing happens to reorganize me out of the picture. I am much too old to start moving.

My best to all our friends in Damascus. I gather that my efforts to throw a bit of business your way from time to time are working out. Just remember to advise me whenever you hear of an opportunity that the Four Rivers Trading Company might use to its advantage. It does not hurt to make the point that the old man Eliezer has not lost his touch.

Finally, a bit of gossip. I think you have met Lot, Abraham's nephew. I have certainly written to you about him. He settled, as I have told you, in a town called Sodom on the shore of the great inland lake. Along with his high intelligence, he is a bit of an opportunist, and while the city's location and its economy offer considerable practical benefits, it is known for its immorality – hardly a place to bring up two young daughters! His wife (please don't quote me) is still the same snoop and tongue-wagger. Abraham is very much the loyal family man (I must have told you about the little military expedition), but he has come to terms with the fact that he cannot expect Lot to amount to much. But that is all right with me. Ishmael, and any child that Sarah may have, are quite enough!

Your loving cousin,

Eliezer

ITEM # 123
FILE ENTRY

Field Report

From: Sodom Area Field Office
To: Administrative Headquarters

Cities of Sodom and Gomorrah, as well as the surrounding towns allied with them, are in utter ruin, with unbelievable loss of life.

Lot, nephew of Abraham, miraculously escaped, along with his wife and two daughters. Before we were able to reach them, an inexplicable accident took the life of his wife. Lot has become paranoid, so afraid of human contact that he has taken his family to hide in a cave in the Judaean hills.

One of our shepherd agents was able to direct Lot and his family to cave #4-32, one of our emergency supply sites. They should be able to hold out for quite some time.

Are there any further instructions?

ITEM # 124
FILE ENTRY

Memorandum

From: Administrative Headquarters

To: Sodom Area Field Office

1. You showed good judgment in giving the support you did to Lot and his daughters.

2. What you have done is quite sufficient. Assume that they can now manage on their own.

3. Remove any remaining supplies from cave #4-32 and abandon it if and when Lot and his daughters vacate it. Find a suitable replacement cave, and transfer the supplies to it.

ITEM # 127
ABRAHAM'S PERSONAL FILE

Progress Report

From: Tekoa Educational Center
To: Abraham

Your son Ishmael continues to make reasonable progress, all things considered, in his studies. We have compared his test results to that of the average thirteen-year old, and conclude as follows:

Mathematical reasoning:	*Outstanding*
Problem solving:	*Average*
Conceptual analysis:	*Slightly above average*
Right and wrong:	*Satisfactory*
Nature skills:	*Fair, at best*

Allow us to emphasize, as we have done before, that our goal is to prepare Ishamael for life and its uncertainties. We realize that your son always travels with a fully staffed caravan. He will certainly make his home in a stable, settled area. Even so, he should have a more than passing acquaintance with astronomical skills, desert lore, botanical and zoological science, water-resource techniques and basic military concepts. At the very least, he is well-advised to be in a position to discuss these matters with those responsible for them intelligently and in an informed fashion.

Within the week, we shall send to you a list of individuals we are prepared to recommend as tutors, and their qualifications. You may already have in your organization most of the requisite knowledge and the ability to teach it. Please do not put this off any longer!

Our faculty has agreed to refer to you for further instruction all matters pertaining to relationship with the female sex, since they bear a logical connection to questions of right and wrong.

As Ishmael reaches the age of thirteen, our faculty recommends that his education be restructured to emphasize interaction within a group setting. We will be pleased to suggest a group here in Tekoa, there is one in Shalem, or we can, if you have a decided preference, establish one in Kiryat Arba. Appropriate subjects will continue to be in the hands of personal tutors.

ITEM # 128
ABRAHAM'S PERSONAL FILE

Medical Evaluation Report

From: Gezer Healing Center
To: Abraham

Our field team has reported to us in detail. The fact that Sarah is pregnant is amazing. We cannot take full credit for this turn of events. Nor can it be explained fully by the herbs you located in Sheba and Hodu.

Now that she is pregnant, we are reluctant to assume full responsibility for her condition. She is, as you very well know, an eighty-nine year old woman, and what we would otherwise describe as normal fourth-month development is not normal for her. She is frail in body, fragile in spirit. A pregnancy, even one so ardently longed-for, makes incredible demands on every part of her being. What can we say – be extremely solicitous of her, and hope for the best.

We propose to monitor her weekly. We recommend frequent and extended periods of bed rest. On a more positive note, at this point, there is absolutely no reason to fear an early termination of her pregnancy.

ITEM # 131
FILE ENTRY

Information Bulletin

To: All Senior Personnel

Sarah has borne a son to Abraham. They are both overjoyed. To them, it is a dream come true. To all of us, it is an occasion for rejoicing.

The name of the newly-born son is Isaac.

Abraham is concerned for Sarah's health, as are all members of Abraham's household. Sarah will nurse Isaac for thirty-one days; after that, we will find a wet-nurse for him.

At the conclusion of this thirty-one day period, Abraham will host a lavish party.

The arrival of this son and heir is a significant event in the annals of our circle here in Hebron, in the affairs of the Four Rivers Trading Company, and especially in the minds and hearts of all who are loyal to the Most High and diligent in the task of spreading the message of the One Creator of heaven and earth.

Schedule festivities as appropriate.

ITEM # 132
FILE ENTRY

Certificate of Eligibility

Young Isaac, aged one month, is hereby designated as an heir to Abraham and a full partner designate in the Four Rivers Trading Company.

He is entitled to any support you can give him, and you are explicitly authorized to employ for his benefit, without limitation, any and all resources at your disposal.

Obviously, he is still a child. Access to files and information is not relevant, nor is the question of when and how to accept direction from him. This and related matters will be addressed in due time.

ITEM # 133
FILE ENTRY

** Confidential **

Confirmation of Eligibility

Eliezer and Eli Hazo, having spoken to Abraham, have determined that he wishes the basic status of Ishmael and Hagar to be unchanged: any support that they may desire is to be extended. Their needs are still a high priority.

It has not yet been clarified what information they are allowed to have access to. Discretion is advised.

There is a very gray area as to accepting direct instructions from them. Exercise extreme caution as to anything beyond personal requests.

ITEM # 135
LETTER FROM ELIEZER TO TUBAL

Dear Tubal,

First of all, I extend to you my heartfelt condolences on the death of your beloved father. Somehow, I always felt closer to him than to any others in our family. As Abraham would say, may the soul of Ra'ama live on as a blessing in our midst.

As I wrote some time ago to your father, Abram and Sarai received a reaffirmation of the One God's pledge to them of a son, to be the next in line to embody the Divine Covenant. It actually took me days and days to get a fuller story of this unearthly vision. Eventually, Abram announced: 'My name is now Abraham. My wife's is now Sarah.' Then, he told us that they will have a son, to be named Isaac. Sarai (now Sarah) true to her manner, declared, 'When he is born, I will decide on a name.'

Within a few more days, and for reasons that even now I just barely understand, every male within Abraham's circle was circumcised. Quite a shock. It took me weeks to get over it!

There was excitement of all kinds. For one thing, I wrote to your father of the kind of place that Abraham's nephew Lot settled in. To make a long story short, that den of iniquity has been wiped off the map. But before that happened, Abraham disappeared for over a day. As it turned out, he was again in seclusion with his mysterious One God. When he showed up again, he acted not unlike a man who has succeeded in a difficult negotiation. At the same time, he seemed to have found an even higher (hard as this is to believe) and more profound level of truth. All he would say to me was: 'Eliezer, I think that for the first time I understand what justice is.' This from a man who has never had an unjust thought.

The real, public, excitement was over Sarah, after so many years, to be pregnant, preparing for motherhood, giving birth, and, at age ninety, nursing a baby! You would have had to be here to appreciate our concern, our joy, and the way events played on our emotions.

I have said many times that I cannot read minds, but I think that anyone can guess the degree of Hagar's consternation and confusion, how the changing situation gradually became clear even to Ishmael, and, above all, how Sarah subsequently reacted. For many of us, and especially for me, it was like walking on eggs. For Abraham, I had a crazy mixture of joy and sympathy. Is his newly-fulfilled dream going to turn into a nightmare? Can the family avoid an explosion?

Abraham now has two sons for whom he has nothing but love. In many ways, it would have been simpler for Abraham if Ishmael had remained his only son. On the other hand, and just between you and me, it is fast becoming obvious to most of us that Ishmael, for all his ability and personal qualities, is not turning out to be the son who can make the central focus of his life that of proclaiming and propagating the faith in the One God.

Can Abraham bring himself to admit such a thing?

Only time will tell.

Your loving cousin,

Eliezer

ITEM # 138
FILE ENTRY

** Confidential **

Priority Dispatch

From: **Administrative Headquarters**
To: **Senior Personnel**

Very serious problems arising here at Hebron. Bad blood between Sarah, Abraham's wife, and Hagar, the woman who bore his firstborn and heir Ishmael. No one is prepared to predict what Abraham will do.

All this tension, not surprisingly, complicates relationships between Ishmael and Isaac, and is reflected among members of their personal staffs.

Anything can happen. Exercise utmost discretion in taking any course of action not specifically authorized that might be interpreted as taking sides, or any denial of support that might be interpreted as disloyalty. We will delineate the course of action to be taken once we receive clear guidelines.

ITEM # 140
LETTER FROM ELIEZER TO TUBAL

Dear Tubal,

When I last wrote to you , I had no way of judging how fast things would move, as the five-way drama of Abraham, Sarah, Hagar, Isaac and Ishmael has been playing itself out. I realized that it would not be easy for Abraham (or for any father) to give up on his first-born son, and to replace Ishmael as his heir, and as successor to all he holds dear.

As a matter of fact, I am now certain that I understood correctly a remark that Abraham let slip, when he finally received the confirmation of the birth of a son to Sarah, to the effect that he actually pleaded with the Most High to leave Ishmael in place as his heir. What can I tell you? It was not to be. Isaac, as you realize, was born. Sarah discovered her own reason for the name Isaac: 'the one who brings laughter.' Sarah persevered in nursing him for a month. Abraham threw a party to end all parties, and every day that lovable child, now two years old, finds a new way to plant joy in our hearts.

In retrospect, I dare say that I must have always realized that there is no way those five could have inhabited one household indefinitely; it is amazing, actually, that the situation lasted as long as it did. Abraham, his great love blinding him to the inevitable and almost obvious, kept trying to reach for a 'peaceful' solution. Sarah, knowing how much Ishmael meant to Abraham, forced herself to bite her tongue day after day. Ishmael, in so many ways still a child, was fully aware that something was not right. Hagar was living an impossible existence; unable to find any kind of parity in this household and unable, or unwilling, to return to the status of 'handmaiden.' Even Isaac's familiar spontaneous laughter retreated before this sea of tension.

Something had to happen, but I did not anticipate what finally occurred. It was a combination of what Sarah resented most, and what neither Abraham nor Sarah could tolerate. Ishmael is the typical big brother. In his natural-born goodness and affection, he shared just about everything with Isaac. He tried to teach him how to hold a bow; he treated him to off-color remarks about women; he brought him all kinds of goodies to eat. Sarah hated having him play the part of big brother but could say nothing.

Then, just two days ago, Ishmael gave Isaac the ultimate gift (actually, to his way of thinking, the supreme compliment): a small idol. It seems that Terah had made and sent to Ishmael's other grandfather, Locum-Re, a pair of incredibly beautiful miniature renditions of the god Ra (shipped, most likely, in one of Abraham's caravans!). Locum-Re sent them to Ishmael, via Hagar, I guess. Ishmael, not surprisingly, prized them immensely, and then, in an overflow of brotherly love, he gave one to Isaac.

Well, an idol is an idol is an idol. It is quite possible that Abraham, if left to his own, would have found some way of working things out, but Sarah saw only one course of action: 'Get that idol-worshipper and his mother out of here,' she commanded.

There was no choice. The two of them were out of here the next morning. I asked Abraham, 'How could you?' His response: 'Trust me.' Knowing Abraham, I do.

Then he added a question: 'Eliezer, define love for me.'

You know something, Tubal, I have no answer for him. It is going to be awfully quiet around here.

If you hear of something happy, write to me.

Your loving cousin,

Eliezer

ITEM # 141
FILE ENTRY

>> Red Alert <<

From: Hebron Headquarters

To: Negev Station #2

Hagar and Ishmael are exiting Hebron by way of the Arad by-pass around Beersheva. Any support at this end must be extremely discreet, and completely covert. Staff did a creditable job of coming up with a plan overnight and briefing two inexperienced travelers on the details.

Hagar and Ishmael have been provided with a four days' supply of food and water. We will make certain that they find a domesticated donkey. This should help them reach Negev Oasis #4-7, which has a good spring and date palms that bear fruit at this time of the year.

Quietly monitor their progress. If need be, find them a better and stronger donkey. From Oasis #4-7, they must get to Sinai Oasis #1-3. You have eight or nine days from today to have in place a fast caravan, which will provide them expedited transportation to Zoan in Egypt.

In addition to the normal traveler's food rations and water skins, and in addition to personal items, Hagar will have two pouches with her. Under no circumstances should she open the blue one. Have your people suggest that the red one look like a money pouch. It is. She is to pay the chief of the caravan the standard hire for expedited transportation. It will leave immediately.

Enclosed herewith is a sealed dispatch case. Note well that it is from Abraham himself, personally. Do not (repeat: do not) open it. Send it on via your fleetest scouts to the house of Locum-Re in Zoan.

Abraham will hold you and Sinai Station #1 personally responsible for the safety and well-being of both Hagar and Ishmael. A word to the wise is sufficient.

ITEM # 142
FILE ENTRY

Field Report

From: Chief, Negev Station #2
To: Hebron Headquarters
Copy to: Administrative Headquarters

Something went terribly wrong! Hagar and Ishmael apparently had difficulty in following the traveling 'suggestions' given to them, perhaps too hurriedly, which were to guide them to Oasis #4-7.

As of early this morning, our contacts at #4-7 were on the lookout for the pair. When by close to midmorning they had not detected any trace of them, they managed to get word to us that something might be amiss.

We pulled out all the stops. Fortunately, it did not take us long to make contact with a scout who had caught sight of them where they were least expected and for us to piece together what had happened. Hagar and Ishmael, two days out, picked the wrong wadi to follow. They wound up at a small outcropping of vegetation a bit north of Oasis #7-11, where, you will recall, we have never had a reliable contact. By then their food and water were exhausted, and so were they. Further instructions given to them for finding water at Oasis #4-7 were obviously useless.

We would have had a disaster on our hands, but for the fact that they somehow ran into a person who Ophir is certain is the same one who met Hagar seventeen years ago when she thought of leaving Abraham's household. We still do not know who he was; he got away from us. Ophir is convinced that the hand of the Most High is evident.

The two were out of food, with only a few last drops of water in their skins; their morale had all but vanished. This 'man' had a more-than-human touch. He led them to the one spot where water could be found. (We have in the interim checked the area out ourselves; there is water present only in that one spot.) She had to dig for the water, but she managed with his help to fill their skins. The boy, mind you – he is now sixteen! – was no help at all.

Two of our scouts talked the two into joining them on the short trek to Oasis #7-11. Our people wheedled and bribed the people at the oasis to send the pair on their way to Negev Oasis #1-3 with enough supplies for five days. I suspect that they will arrive in four days out of water. I also guarantee you that they will now keep 'bumping into' all sorts of travelers so that we will be sure that they get there in one piece.

As they say: All in a day's work! We will not be able to assess the impact on staffing all along the line for at least a week, but at least mother and son are out of harm's way.

ITEM # 143
FILE ENTRY

Field Report

From: Chief, Sinai Station #1
To: Administrative Headquarters

The woman Hagar and the lad Ishmael were trailed with great care by Negev Station #2's crack scout unit. There is a slight chance they were detected. However, the station chief felt that, considering all that had happened to them in the previous four days, avoidance of detection was less important than the safety of the pair.

Allow us to explain. Hagar and Ishmael, as we have been given to understand, were told very few details of the arrangements for their relocation, partly because of the hurried nature of their departure and partly because it was deemed that they would not be able to take in the complete picture. Yet, they should have known not to expect to find water until they got to Oasis #4-7. They reached somewhat of an outcropping of vegetation, and had no inkling of how to locate the water that made it possible. If not the woman, then at least a son of Abraham should have had enough presence of mind and initiative to investigate and enough skill to find water. They gave us the impression of having given up.

Ophir will have told you of this strange man, and of his role in restoring her morale and leading her to water. Where Abraham and his family are concerned, wonders never cease!

We have taken it on ourselves to give instructions to the scout accompanying the caravan from Sinai Oasis #1-3 to Zoan to begin a process of vigorous education of Ishmael, son of Abraham, in the secrets of desert survival. He will eventually have to know all that we know, and (if I may presume to offer an opinion) should have learned much of it before now. If he is Abraham's son, he is our son, and he will be schooled accordingly.

We assume you will relay to Abraham all that we have reported.

We have shared with Negev Station #2 as much of this report as they need to know.

ITEM # 144
FILE ENTRY

Letter of Commendation

From: Administrative Headquarters

To: Negev Station #2

Abraham desires us to commend you on the efficient and caring way in which you have seen to the needs of Hagar and Ishmael. Your initiative in responding to unforeseen circumstances as they unfolded impresses him.

Please advise us directly and promptly, without waiting for your monthly report, if any of your resources expended on their behalf need replenishing.

If you can do so without being too obvious about it, try once more to find out about this person who befriended Hagar. He was not one of our people, nor anyone with whom we have contact. We have every confidence that you could have done as well, but when help arrives from an unbidden direction, it is best to know its source and its name. It can hardly be a coincidence.

ITEM # 145
FILE ENTRY

Letter of Commendation

From: Administrative Headquarters

To: Sinai Station #1

Abraham wishes us to commend you on the efficient and caring manner in which you have received, and in turn sent on to Egypt, both Hagar and Ishmael. Your solicitude and initiative will not be forgotten.

He concurs in your decision to reinforce Ishmael's knowledge of desert lore.

ITEM # 148
LETTER FROM ABRAHAM TO TERAH

Dear Father,

You will be hearing from various sources many differing slants – some even judgmental – on the events of these past few weeks. I owe it to you to give you a bit of insight into what really happened, or at least into how I personally perceive my actions, and the reactions of those about me.

I may be trying too hard to put a good face on what on the surface presents itself as an act of cruelty, namely removing my own son Ishmael and his mother Hagar from the circle of our family here in Hebron. Please hear me out. It only makes sense if I put things in context.

You were at the center of the discussions that included Sarah and me, Sarah's grandmother and mother, and my mother, and which concluded with Sarah – then Sarai – and me marrying. All the arguments, pro and con, are history, but we did agree to a number of things, one of which was that in our household there would never be any compromise or dilution of our great principle of One God, Who created heaven and earth, Who is the great Mover behind human history, and Who teaches us right and wrong. In some ways, Sarah is more of a stickler for this principle than I am, but I will come to that. We also agreed that I would never have another wife during Sarah's lifetime. And third, Sarai pledged herself to accompany me wherever life would lead me.

It is clear that despite all our planning, we failed to foresee one problem: the fact that Sarah and I would be childless for so long. Think of it: over twenty years in Ur, almost twenty-five in Kharran, and then ten years in Canaan. Sarah and I had always assumed that a child or children of ours would perpetuate this central vision in our lives. Hopefully, that assumption has now become fact, but let us not skip over too lightly events that took place in the interim.

It is not quite accurate to say that we consulted you, but it is a fair statement that you were aware of every step leading to our decision that it was better that a son be born who was my child, even if not Sarah's, than that I have no heir at all. Hagar became my second wife. We all three agreed that 'number two' was to be an unequivocally accurate description of Hagar's status, but human nature is such that a woman who is pregnant will have feelings of having outshone a woman who cannot conceive, and cannot help flaunting them. Especially if the pregnant woman is Hagar, and the mistress is Sarah. I could not anticipate Hagar's flaunting, but I certainly should have predicted Sarah's reaction. Suffice it to say that it was easy for Sarah to make Hagar want to leave. That Hagar eventually returned, for sixteen years as it turned out, is all but unbelievable, but return and stay she did.

Hagar returned. Ishmael was born. Ishmael was reared as my son and heir. It was easier for Sarah than for me to perceive the negative qualities in his character and nature. Even I must now admit that Ishmael was not and is not the appropriate candidate for continuing the vision and project that has driven Sarah and me for some seventy years. Deep down, I knew this, but as long as he was my only child, I hoped against hope that he would somehow grow into this vision and make our dream his own.

After Isaac was born, it became clear that the principal mover in disseminating our vision of the One God would not be Ishmael. On the other hand (strictly between us for now) he can be and will be groomed for some of the many other things for which I can best rely on a family member, such as the Four Rivers Trading Company.

Sarah, as I said, was more sensitive than I to Ishmael's deficiencies, and managed to mention them in various casual ways, but never made an issue of his status until Isaac was born. At that point, she made it crystal clear that to her, Isaac and Ishmael were not brothers. And so she registered her objection to Ishmael's trying to play the role of big brother.

This would not have swayed me, I am sure. But then something happened out of the blue. Ishmael had had for some time two of your depictions, lovely I must admit, of the god Ra. We never made an issue of it; after all, they were a gift from his other grandfather. But one fine morning, we found one of these idols in the hands of Isaac. It was, in Isaac's own words, 'a sign of his bond to his big brother.'

Sarah and I both hit the roof. After the initial shock, I was of a mind to try to smooth it over, but Sarah would have none of it. 'This idol-loving servant-girl's son,' she shouted, 'will not be a joint heir with my son Isaac!'

Not you, not I, not anyone could have made headway against Sarah's determination. I communed with God. I interceded for Ishmael in every way I could. The answer was unambiguous: 'Sarah is your wife; whatever she says, you must do.'

Fortunately, I have all kinds of resources. When I need them, they can be used. Ishmael is out of my household in Hebron, but not out of my heart.

You will receive copies of detailed reports from our Administrative Headquarters that will explain in detail that the time has come to place Ishmael's training in the hands of others. Together with his mother Hagar, he will be in Zoan, by the time this reaches you, and from there he will be guided by his Egyptian grandfather Locum-Re. Please get a message to Ishmael from time to time, but please do not send him any more idols.

I am sure that you will hear from Sarah before long, if you have not already! Just remember: Sarah knows only that I sent Hagar and Ishmael packing with less than what one donkey can carry, which gave them a lot to haul on their backs that first morning. Take my word for it, there is no way they could get lost or be without access to food and water. I hope the day will come when I can tell Sarah, but for now it is our secret.

Your loving son,

Abraham

ITEM # 150
FILE ENTRY

Confirmation of Eligibility

From: Administrative Headquarters

To: Director of Operations/Egypt

You have received bits and pieces of information as to what is happening to Ishmael and Hagar. The staffs of the various areas they have passed through these past three weeks will have competently served them. Now the time has come to do what field units cannot do.

They will arrive in the area administered by your headquarters, and then you will commence the intricate task of introducing them to all aspects of your operation.

Abraham has confirmed that you are to treat Ishmael as heir and partner. When he reaches the age of twenty, we anticipate that he will gradually be authorized to make decisions and participate in policy councils. Long before then, he is to have access to information; you will take steps to make certain the he knows everything that you know – everything that there is to know. Be sure not to treat him as a child.

From time to time, messages will come from Abraham to Ishmael. He is to see them immediately. Only if he so chooses, will he share all or parts of their content with you.

ITEM # 151
FILE ENTRY

>> Priority Message <<

From: Administrative Headquarters

To: Zoan Office

Hagar the Egyptian and her son Ishmael, son of Abraham, will shortly be arriving in Zoan. We call to your attention previous messages entitling them to draw on your resources and to call on you for assistance as needed. They will arrive tired and in depressed spirits. Abraham wishes you to extend yourselves on their behalf exactly as you would on his behalf.

Alert our friend Locum-Re without delay, and inform him immediately on their arrival. Be aware that Hagar is his daughter and that Ishmael is his grandson. He will want to be part of the day-to-day management of their affairs, but you will retain full responsibility for the two of them. Ishmael will in due course be a partner in the Four Rivers Trading Company. (Be advised that you may in the not too distant future be receiving your orders from him.)

Hagar will arrive with two pouches. The red one contains money; if it is depleted, offer to advance to her any money she may require. The blue one contains letters. Hagar was told not to open it, but as she arrives in Egypt she should see the contents. You, of course, can only suggest, but Abraham wishes her and Ishmael to see the letters before Locum-Re calls for them. Do not ask her any questions about the contents. She will probably choose not to speak to you of them.

Finally, some parts of Ishmael's education have been deferred, and for much too long. Now, even if he feels it is difficult at times, he is to be thoroughly grounded in everything that is in the power of any member of your staff to teach him.

ITEM # 153
LETTER FROM ABRAHAM TO HAGAR

Dear Hagar,

Some day you will realize that all this is for the best. I think you will concede that at each step my choices were limited. At the risk of being overly blunt, allow me to remind you that from the very beginning, I have tried to convey unambiguously to you and to your father (and my friend) that I have only one wife and that her name is Sarah.

Without question, we are both equally proud of Ishmael's development. I do not deny that, had he remained my only son, he would have been my sole heir, in every respect. But the Almighty has willed differently. Isaac will in time be my principal heir, charged with spreading my One God vision far and wide.

Nevertheless, Ishmael remains my son, and my heir. As he matures, I look forward to giving him ever-increasing responsibility and authority in my Four Rivers Trading Company. It is quite possible that Isaac will dedicate his attention to the message to which he is born, and that central roles in the leadership of our trading company will be assigned to Ishmael and our cousins in Ur and Kharran.

Enclosed is a list of our affiliates. They have express orders to provide you anything that you require, and to intercede for you as needed. Any of them will transmit faithfully and expeditiously any messages you have for me. Never hesitate to remind any of them that what they do for you, they do for

Ishmael, and what they do for Ishmael, they do for Abraham.

My resources make distances shrink, but not disappear. Make sure that Ishmael realizes that my feelings for him are undiminished. Some day he will be able to occupy a place that is rightfully his. (When that happens, rest assured, you will be at his side.) Again, if you need anything, ask.

With highest regard,

Abraham

ITEM # 154
LETTER FROM ABRAHAM TO LOCUM-RE

Dear Locum-Re,

What I feared has happened. Hagar and Ishmael can no longer remain in my household here in Hebron. Without going into details, life has changed for me as well, but more of that another time.

Take my word for it, I could send no one with them on the first leg of their journey to join you in Egypt. I was able to detail a trusted scout, the best available on such short notice (one who knows how to protect himself and others and knows how to be at the same time invisible) to shadow them.

The itinerary set for them is via Negev Oasis #4-7, thence to Sinai Oasis #1-3, and from there with a fast caravan to Zoan. You should be contacted as soon as they arrive, and then there can be little if anything that they require that is beyond your ability to provide. Ishmael is my child; draw from my people in his name anything that you need.

I have some hope that Hagar's joy of reunion with family and friends after an absence of some twenty years will take some of the edge off the hurt of leaving us in Hebron, but it will take a long while. Please do your best; I fear that she is close to the breaking point.

Forgive me if I repeat myself, but believe me, Locum-Re, Ishmael remains my son. You, however, are there with him, and you are his grandfather. Help him to stay in touch with the Four Rivers operation, and to learn from its people all he can of the ways both of the desert and of the settled world. For their part they all understand that he is entitled to any resources at their command, but more so to information and expertise at their disposal. He should be encouraged to call on them with absolutely no hesitation.

Exhort him as well to learn all he can from your Egyptian friends, and from whoever you feel has wisdom to impart. Convince them to be open and sharing with him.

Please keep me posted on the welfare and progress of Ishmael and Hagar.

Fraternally yours,

Abraham

ITEM # 155
LETTER FROM ABRAHAM TO ISHMAEL

Dear Ishmael,

Things have moved much too fast in the past few days. You, of all people, do not need to be told of the state that Sarah has been in for some time now. We both remember her tantrums at seeing you playing with Isaac who is, when all is said and done, your brother. Yet, we could have worked things out. Your unforgivable deed was giving Isaac an idol. I hope that you now understand how it agitated Sarah and me.

Realistically speaking, and with the gift of hindsight, I probably should have acted sooner to move you in the direction of independence. I have done so now. By the time you see this letter you will have been reunited with Locum-Re, who after all is your grandfather. You will also have experienced the realities of travel. Give it some thought; realize that the 'good fortune' that has enabled you to reach Egypt has been due to many people assisting your mother and yourself out of loyalty to me.

Remember all those you have met, for you may very well need them again. They have been reminded that you are a son of Abraham. You can turn to them for what you need, and they will be forthcoming; but don't be surprised if they make you do things for yourself. They will be teaching you to be self-reliant, and to deal with all sorts of people and with both desert and city life. There is no doubt in my mind that your trek from Hebron to Egypt will have awakened you to how much there is for you to learn.

Let me again make a point of reminding you that you are a son of Abraham. All that you grew up with and all that you have observed since you left Hebron came into being because the Most High has been with me. It will not be easy to live in accordance with His teachings in Egypt, but I call on you to be mindful always that there is but One God, the One Who created heaven and earth. I pray to Him daily to protect you, and to fulfill His promise to make of you a mighty nation.

As things stand, you cannot get back to Hebron in the foreseeable future, and I think it wiser that for the time being I not be seen in Egypt. However, as you know, I go out from time to time traveling with one of my caravans. Before long, I hope that we shall meet at one of the oases in the Negev.

More than that: I look forward to the day when you can assume an active role in the conduct of my commercial affairs. Since it is what you have shown a bent for, it is what I want for you.

I impress on you that you have now reached the point where you should begin to accept a degree of responsibility for your mother's welfare. Between those allied with me, and the resources of her father, Locum-Re, she should lack for nothing material, but the comfort of a child is worth more than things we can make or buy.

From afar, I wish you all the best. I hope to hear from you regularly. Those who brought you to Zoan, and our affiliates whom you will be seeing, can and will carry messages with security. They will teach you all you need to know, and when we meet I will confirm your progress.

Your loving father,

Abraham

ITEM # 156
LETTER FROM HAGAR TO ABRAHAM

Dear Abraham,

I am just beginning to put the pieces together. Things moved so suddenly and so horribly.

The fact that the two beautiful icons that Ishmael treasured were really idols never registered on me. What seemed important was that they were that rare thing: a memento of both his grandfathers. And you said nothing, either. So I saw nothing wrong in Ishmael's impulsive gift of one of them to his beloved baby brother Isaac. When reality struck, it was too late.

You cannot deny that the decision to throw Ishmael out of your household was heartless. The overnight implementation was so sudden! We were rousted out of bed before dawn, loaded up with all kinds of strange objects and I don't know how many kikars of food and water.

I never knew how one travels through the desert. Ishmael sort of knew, in theory, but was overwhelmed by the details. To give but one example (and an almost fatal one at that): we in our innocence were delighted to observe that the more we ate, the lighter the load we had to carry. As a result, we were parched and starving when we got to a small clump of shrubbery in the middle of the desert. We were too ignorant to know that this could not be the oasis mentioned in the travel instructions so hurriedly given us. All we knew was that the sketch said, 'Here is a well,' and there was no well. To be perfectly honest, if I felt rejected when we received our marching orders, I now felt abandoned. I had this nagging feeling that we might have been intentionally misdirected. Of course, a sixteen-year-old who has lived his entire life with caravan types should have known about oases – but neither of us was in any condition to examine a bunch of undergrowth to trace its source of water. Then this apparition materialized out of nowhere, pointed and started digging. He made Ishmael finish digging and had me fill a skin with water. I didn't care at that moment whether your God sent him, or whether he was one of your employees, or even a stranger.

Soon after, we started running into helpful sorts wherever we turned. (It really started, now that my eyes are open, the very first afternoon, when some vagrant talked us into taking his spare donkey, and then said, 'I know who you are; I'll collect from Abraham.') Everywhere we have run into people who seem to know Abraham, and are more than happy to lend a hand to Abraham's kin. The more I think about it, the more I realize it has been no coincidence.

We are now bumping along on a fast caravan to Zoan. As anxious as I am to see my father and enter a civilized house, I wish they would move more slowly and more smoothly.

These few days have brought me and Ishmael closer together. They have also opened my eyes to a simple fact: Ishmael has been a pampered, spoiled brat. He refused to look out for himself. I realize that this came from having everything handed to him.

Realizing that we have not been abandoned makes me hopeful that you will find a way of reaching out to your son. Meanwhile, Ishmael is not going to be pampered any longer. He is now going to learn to stand on his own two feet like the man I want him to be, and the man he has to be. Unless I miss my guess, it is the kind of man you want him to be as well.

When I get to Father's house, I will have him write to you, and I will keep you up to date on our son's progress.

Faithfully yours,

Hagar

ITEM # 157
LETTER FROM HAGAR TO ELIEZER

Dear Eliezer,

I have already written to your master about events that befell Ishmael and me in recent days. Even as I write, Ishmael and I are being whisked to Egypt and to exile in my father's house. Please excuse me, but I have to share with someone my feelings about the man I will always know as Abram.

I was little more than a child when Father placed me in the household of 'that Hebrew.'

I liked Sarah, and I enjoyed working for her, but I came to adore Abram. I had grown up thinking that I would never care for any male, but Abram unknowingly changed all that.

Then, when they had no children for so long, came my grand opportunity. Sarai (I guess I must call her Sarah) has always looked at me as less than her equal in any way. Imagine my amazement when she suggested that I bear a child for Abram! Don't ask how my heart pounded. In my fantasy, those few months, until I knew I was pregnant, were one long honeymoon.

Abraham, wrapped up as he was with the objective of procreating an heir to carry on the mission of bringing the world closer to the Most High, probably did not realize then, and may not realize now, what it has meant to me as a woman. But Sarah did, and does. To you, it can be no surprise that, more than she wanted Ishmael out of her house, she wanted me out of the picture. Now she has had her way.

But that is the smaller part of this story. If I felt abandoned, Ishmael felt betrayed. I was forced to realize that I had no inalienable claim on Abram; Ishmael was and is unshaken in his belief that he does.

Then, when we were ousted from Abram's house, a simple misreading of a map (I will come to that) brings us, not to an oasis, but to the merest pinpoint of vegetation. At that moment, Ishmael was sure that the father who had expressed his love for him all these years had effectively replaced him with Isaac, and done it in an underhanded and cruel fashion. Can you blame him for feeling abandoned and betrayed? Can you fault him for being unable to act?

You will know without my telling you how, in spite of our bungling, things worked out. We are now on our way.

One of the scouts deployed to this caravan that 'just happened' to be at Sinai Oasis #1-3, when we arrived, is a born teacher. He has been assigned to take Ishmael under his wing, and he lets me sit in on the lessons. The very first session was an exercise in map reading. We showed him the map that was shoved into our hands that last hour in Hebron, and he explained to us how to read it. We easily remembered exactly where we went astray. Then he jogged our memory further to make us realize that there were little signs that could have told us where a real oasis (even though not the one on our map) lay.

Eliezer, ask yourself why Ishmael could not read a map straight, why he could not see at once that the place we had come to was not the place described, why he could not figure out that any vegetation implies water somewhere near. It was partly due to his own indolence. He was pampered and spoiled and given his own way too much. He failed to apply himself to what did not appeal to him. I am writing to Abram (I should say Abraham, shouldn't I?) and telling him that Ishmael will be pampered no more, but he should never have been so pampered in the first place.

You are Abram's most trusted assistant, senior in service and in reliability. If Abram will listen to anyone, he will listen to you. Ishmael is now in good hands. Between my father and myself we will make a man out of him.

It is really none of my business, and I don't know why I should worry myself about him, but somehow I like little Isaac. The poor child has the same Abram for a father and an unstable, aged Sarah for a mother. Someone has to convince Abram that he must not pamper this boy also. Please try your best to get through to him.

Ishmael and I will be all right. Life is strange; you and I may see each other again. I hope so. Whether we do or not, use Abram's contacts to get in touch with your old friend. Please let me know how Abram is doing. I don't know why, but I still wish him all the best.

May life be kind to you, Eliezer.

Yours in friendship,

Hagar

ITEM # 161
FILE ENTRY

Progress Report

From: Zoan Field Office

To: Administrative Headquarters

The young man Ishmael – for so we feel we may call him – has made progress beyond our expectations. His improvement in the following areas is noteworthy:

(1) Re: knowledge of the lands and peoples of the Four Rivers area:
More than satisfactory.

(2) Re: mastery of the lore of the desert:
Almost amazing, for one reared in the more settled areas.
(Ratings do not apply to such as him, but he would easily qualify as a scout, second rank.)

(3) Re: acquaintance with the methods of our enterprise:
Quite adequate. He exhibits more interest than we would expect of someone his age.

Two additional items. He reveals more than a passing curiosity of the being he calls the Most High. This must refer to a legacy he has brought with him from Abraham's house. Please advise.

Finally, he will be assigned as caravan-leader-in-training to the second autumn caravan to Sinai Oasis #1-3. Please report this to Abraham. As we recall, his last two inspections of our Sinai oases were scheduled in the autumn.

ITEM # 164
ABRAHAM'S JOURNAL

MEDICAL EVALUATION REPORT

From: Gezer Healing Center
To: Abraham

Our staff has completed its evaluation of the results of our examinations of Sarah and yourself.

You, Abraham, are in excellent health for a man past the age of one hundred. You should continue so for many years to come.

We wish we could say the same for Sarah. Hers is a difficult case. First, she has never fully rebounded from the physical toll that childbirth exacted from her. She insists on doing more than she should for her son Isaac. Additionally, our impression is that she continues to labor under a burden of guilt for having forced Ishmael, your firstborn, out of the house.

You must watch her carefully.

ITEM # 167
ABRAHAM'S JOURNAL

Status Update

From: Chief, Egyptian District
To: Abraham

It is now almost two years that Ishmael, along with his mother Hagar, has been domiciled in Egypt.

To begin with, he has taken to all we have asked him to learn as a fish takes to water.

Beyond this, he shows an uncommon ability to relate to people, from senior officials in our Four Rivers Trading Company and high ranking members of the Pharaoh's court, to the lowliest of our camel drivers and storehouse attendants. Most unusual in someone not quite eighteen.

Even more remarkable, he demonstrates a totally unexpected strong interest in the total picture, and even some grasp of strategic planning.

Despite reports which surface continually of friction accompanying his move to this area, we hear nothing negative on this score from Ishmael himself.

We must confess that the rigorous agenda we have set for him allows him but little occasion to concern himself with further study of the One Most High. We are open to your suggestions.

ITEM # 173
FILE ENTRY

Memorandum

From: Administrative Headquarters, Sinai District

To: All Personnel

A team personally headed by Abraham will conduct the upcoming annual inspection of the Negev and Sinai districts. It will conclude with a celebration on the day of the autumn full moon. We are confident that you will all see to it that the inspection produces no negative results that might mar the festivities.

Young Ishmael, who will reach his eighteenth birthday at that time, will attend. The celebration will note this milestone.

Hagar, Ishmael's mother, will naturally be on hand for her son's birthday party. Since she will in a sense be hosting Abraham, she may make special requests of us. Take care to try to anticipate anything that any of the three may require.

It is quite possible that Abraham will bring along the child Isaac, now four years old, to spend some time with his brother. Alert one or two families with small children to provide appropriate amenities.

ITEM # 174
FILE ENTRY

>> Confidential <<

From: Chief, Administrative Headquarters

To: Chief, Zoan Field Office

Copies to: Chiefs – Egyptian, Sinai & Negev Districts

You are aware that the forthcoming Annual Inspection of the Sinai District will be an unusual event.

The cast of characters: Abraham and Isaac, Ishmael and Hagar, calls for utmost attention to both security and comfort.

You will note that Sarah will not be among those attending. Be very discreet as to what information gets back to Hebron. Search out a quantity of gifts suitable for a young boy, which will give Isaac more than enough to speak of to his mother. Of course, you will see that Abraham has a profusion of gifts to bring back to Sarah.

One final – and highly confidential – item: We believe, now that Ishmael is turning eighteen, that Abraham and Hagar will agree it is time for him to be married. Do a thorough check of all prospective brides, first with all available background information in your files, next with Locum-Re, then with Hagar and Ishmael, and finally with Abraham.

ITEM # 177
LETTER FROM HAGAR TO TERAH

Dear Terah,

I hope that I can presume to share with you a bit of my thinking, and, so to speak, my justification for a decision that I have taken upon myself. If you concur in my thinking, it will be a great service to me – and even more so to your grandson Ishmael – if word of the decision comes to Abraham through you.

For any number of reasons, it seemed best at the time, and almost certainly *was* best in the short run, for Ishmael and myself to opt for the relative quiet and enhanced security of my father's house in Zoan.

Now, mostly for the good, Ishmael has a mind of his own. He has his heart set on moving to the Paran area. I think I know what is driving him. Quite naturally, he has a deep need (you understand why) to prove he can now master a desert wilderness area. By now, I am satisfied that he can, with standard everyday support. Just as understandably, he is bent on setting up conditions that will afford him the opportunity to see his father more frequently. (I can't quite yet get up the courage to tell my own father that it will not be too long before I am ready to make the same move. I am not all that far from forgiving Abraham for bending under the pressure to which Sarah subjected him.) Paran, as you must know, is really one caravan-stage from Hebron, and can now be reached from Beersheva in one day and one night. (I am sure you know all about Negev Oases #4-7 and #7-11; I for one will never forget!)

Frankly, as far as I can gather, my son is anxious to establish himself as 'his own man.' It seems we have found a bride who suits him and is acceptable to his father, his grandfather and myself. I wish she could meet you. Perhaps Ishmael himself will fill you in.

I am sure that Abraham has written to you about the eighteenth birthday party. It was a success on all counts. I even found myself taking a liking to Isaac. (After all, none of this was his fault.)

We sometimes speculate, 'What if?' What if Ishmael and I had never left Hebron? Life would have been quieter, and there would have been fewer hard feelings. Realistically, though, I would still be Sarah's personal attendant (albeit a respected one, hopefully) and Ishmael might have remained a spoiled brat with no responsibilities other than to learn about the universe and to reflect on humanity's place in it. Please don't ask me what I would have preferred. We cannot, in any event, turn the clock back; we can only learn from events and with luck turn them to our advantage.

Now, it is time to move forward. If Ishmael wants Paran – so be it. He can probably do more from there than sitting here in Zoan. Don't be surprised if a caravan leader shows up at your tent in Kharran with a letter written by Ishmael.

Finally, thank you for having a son with so many admirable qualities. I honestly feel I am the better off for having known him.

With highest esteem,

Hagar 'the Egyptian'

ITEM # 181
FILE ENTRY

Internal Memorandum

Background information

From: Chief of Staff – Abraham's Hebron Household

To: Senior Staff

Our normal concerns are with administrative and logistic matters, but to properly serve the interests of Abraham and his family, we must all be aware of what motivates them.

The travels of Abraham and Isaac to a variety of locations continue. Isaac shows unusual sensitivity for a lad barely six years old. It is amazing to hear the words that come from his mouth.

Sarah, who is almost never able to leave her tent, is alternately the doting mother who cannot bear to see her son torn from her and the proud mother who delights in having him describe to her places he has been and things he has seen and heard. The vicarious pleasure that his reports bring her is all the pleasure she needs – or at least all that her physical condition can tolerate.

The only additional delight she looks forward to is the occasional flash of insight that Isaac shares with her. We think that his spiritual development, as it slowly but visibly unfolds, brings even more pleasure to Sarah than to Abraham, who has his more active and more intense speculations to stimulate him, and who is, of course, busy with a much greater variety of activity.

Isaac's formal education, under the guidance of the Tekoa Educational Center, will no doubt begin shortly.

ITEM # 182
ABRAHAM'S PERSONAL FILE

Evaluation Report

From: *Tekoa Educational Center*
To: *Abraham*

Your son Isaac, as you know, is a most unusual lad. No conventional report card can do him justice. His instructors and I have collaborated on this narrative style of a report on his progress.

Our Evaluation and Testing people have met with Isaac and are thrilled with their findings. Isaac is a very intelligent, highly sensitive lad. At the age of six, he exhibits sparks of insight and reasoning ability that some people never achieve. We also find his level of concern for other people, for animals and even for plant life to be very much deeper than we would expect.

If anything, he is too serious for such a young child. Encourage his mother to cuddle him, and urge him to play more.

By the way, he dropped a remark about missing his brother. Please fill us in on any possibly helpful details.

ITEM # 198
ABRAHAM'S PERSONAL FILE

Progress Report

From: Tekoa Educational Center

To: Abraham

Isaac, now ten years old, continues to make solid progress. He does well in all his formal subjects, and is constantly challenging his instructors to come up with something new.

His fixation on the idea of devotion to the Most High disconcerts us. One member of our staff or another can readily answer most of the youngster's questions, but he has come up with one question with which we all have difficulty. He wants to know how a person can be sure that he is doing all he can in the service of the One God. We all, of course, want to do what is right, we tell him; yet we have a right to live our lives with moderate regard for personal comfort and with reasonable attention to personal fulfillment. At times he gives the impression that he cannot reconcile these two ideas, that it frustrates him that he cannot 'know' that he is serving his God fully. At the appropriate time, you will have to help him sort this out yourself.

We feel he is ready to be introduced to a wider, more panoramic view of life. He often focuses his attention on connections. If you agree that it is justified, we will call in a team of wise men who have studied in a more structured manner the complex relationships and interdependence of the land, vegetation, animal life and humans. He is the first student we have ever had who we are confident will fathom their thinking.

ITEM # 201
FILE ENTRY

Certificate of Eligibility

From: Administrative Headquarters

To: All Senior Personnel

Ishmael, son of Abraham, has two sons, Nebaiot and Kedar; as well as a daughter, named Mahalat. They and any additional children born to him in the future are eligible for routine support from all appropriate resources.

Much of their needs will be supplied as a matter of course by their maternal great-grandfather Locum-Re. It is recommended that you coordinate with him.

Inform this headquarters, as well as the Zoan and Sinai districts, of any unusual requirements. We will advise you.

ITEM # 210
FILE ENTRY

From: Eshkol

To: Hebron District Headquarters

Copy to: Administrative Headquarters

Eshkol, although not on our staff, is a confidant and adviser of Abraham of long standing. Abraham values his advice.

You will be interested to hear my reading of the latest, most intriguing turn of events. I am referring to the expedition, two days before the autumn new moon, on which Isaac turned thirteen. Abraham, in sharp contrast to previous outings with Isaac, traveled with him to a lonely peak in the hills east of Hebron, the area pock-marked with caves. As you are aware, in addition to the normal provisions for a four or five day trip, they took a choice lamb, a large bundle of kindling, an urn containing fire and a knife of striking design.

Your own scouts, of course, would never dream of allowing Abraham (or Isaac, for that matter) out of their sight. Normally, routine security efforts would more than suffice, but something about the arrangements hinted that an extraordinary occurrence was in the making. I have numbered Abraham among my friends for thirty-six years now, and an aura of mystery hung in the air. I decided to shadow them personally.

For two days they traveled with but two attendants. At frequent intervals, they stopped. Bit by bit (he will have to forgive me for overhearing much of what was spoken!), Abraham and

Isaac spoke about belief in God, the duty of a human being to serve that God wholeheartedly, and the obligation to ensure that there will be those who will serve the Most High tomorrow and many tomorrows to come.

Towards evening of the second day, they left the attendants behind, climbed a tall hill, built an altar and offered up the lamb as a burnt offering. Abraham returned with a satisfied look on his face; Isaac was all aglow, in a discomfiting, eerie fashion. He seemed to have undergone a spiritual experience of extreme intensity.

Sarah, who had risen early to send them on their way, waited up for them (both actions unusual for her) late into the evening of the fourth day. They were up through the night, talking and talking, hardly eating.

ITEM # 222
ABRAHAM'S PERSONAL FILE

Progress Report

From: Headmaster, Tekoa Educational Center

To: Abraham

Isaac continues to make solid progress. As we would expect of a fifteen-year-old, he has concentrated his interest in certain directions, with a correspondingly low level of attention to others.

First and foremost: his annual pilgrimages to the cave-filled hill area are constantly on his mind. He is fascinated by the concept of the burnt offering as a symbol of unconditional service to the One God. Our counseling staff suspect an undertone of a desire to make of himself such an offering, as a supreme attestation of loyalty. You are our authority on belief in the Most High and service to Him; we feel it would be most appropriate for you to take personal charge of this area of Isaac's development.

Isaac has developed a real flair for anything connected with agriculture. He loves the land, and delights in digging into it. He has actually come up with some original thoughts on irrigation, and is absorbed in finding novel ways to improve yields. He has, as well, taken with enthusiasm to animal husbandry, and is fascinated by a new concept called selective breeding.

On the other hand, aside from a passable competence in accounting concepts, he shows a disappointingly low level of interest in the principles of commerce and related aspects of geography. For example, he has trouble remembering where Kharran, his own grandfather's home, is located. Nor can he call to mind what the various countries in our area produce or consume.

ITEM # 236
LETTER FROM ABRAHAM TO ISHMAEL

Dear Ishmael,

In two days, you turn thirty. Your progress and advancement have always been important to me, but I have been careful to promote you only to that level for which you have demonstrated competence. My patience – not to mention yours – has now, I am happy and proud to assert, been proven justified. Every one of our administrators concurs, enthusiastically, in your selection as chief of the new Southwest Trust.

You are obviously now responsible for a great deal:

(1) Transportation, including (but not limited to) caravans.
(2) Communications within the Southwestern area and between it and other areas.
(3) Acquisition of merchandise suitable for sale within your area and abroad.
(4) Marketing in the area under your jurisdiction.
(5) Joint operations with the Canaan, Lebanon, Damascus and Chaldaean areas.
(6) Maintaining ongoing relationships with oases and related facilities.
(7) Expanding the level of our cooperation with the Philistines.

Your regular reports will be submitted to Administrative Headquarters, and normal instructions will come through that channel.

There are some things, though, you should bring directly to me. First, try to work out a model for integrated long-haul caravans to transport people and valuable shipments directly from point to point. I will work on this project with you personally.

This will help with another concern of mine. Our family is growing. Looking out for their safety is an increasingly real concern for me, and I am asking you to make it yours. See every caravan as a pair of eyes and a ready helping hand. Share with me directly all that you do in that direction.

Again, in closing, may I reiterate my deep sense of pride in how far you have come in your personal development. I look forward to great things from you.

Your loving Father,

Abraham

ITEM # 237
ITEM ENTRY

Reorganization Plan

From: Abraham

To: All Units

Effective immediately, the Egyptian, Sinai and Negev district offices are combined into a newly-created regional division, to be known as the Southwest Trust. This new entity will, in addition, assume primary responsibility for dealings with the Philistine cities.

The Trust will oversee commercial operations, including caravans, oases and other caravan facilities, purchasing, marketing and associated contracting.

Agricultural and animal ranching activities or other food production concerns are not included in the operations of the Trust.

Also effective immediately, Ishmael is appointed chief of the Southwest Trust.

Announcements of appointments, areas of responsibility and chains of command will be issued in due course by Ishmael.

ITEM # 239
LETTER FROM ABRAHAM TO ISHMAEL

Dear Ishmael,

I have outlined for you what I expect of you, in regards both to family and to the Four Rivers Trading Company. I now must add a very special request. There is no one else I can turn to. Isaac is dear to both of us, and is the apple of Sarah's eye. I know that your feelings toward Sarah are ambivalent, to say the least. But, now that you are married, you can understand that to me she is more precious than anyone else, dearer than my soul. For her sake and for his own, Isaac is the concern of all of us, and his safety is our highest priority. He has a tendency to wander off alone. Normally, I would not worry about a youngster of almost sixteen. If nothing else, this is appropriate for one who always has farming, animal husbandry and water resources on his mind, and is on the lookout for ways to coordinate them. Nevertheless, we must watch over him, especially when he takes off in search of one more clue to the will of the Most High.

Isaac may not know, but you and I know, that in the desert survival depends on instinct, and on friends as well. He may sometimes, through lack of instinct, be oblivious to where he is; we must be his friends and make certain that this does not lead to his being lost.

In this vein, I share a secret with you. Isaac is totally absorbed in a desire to constantly demonstrate his unconditional devotion to the Most High. I have devoted the major part of my life and a significant portion of my resources to His service. I think I can honestly say (and so can you, I daresay) that I have helped spread the word of the existence of One God, and have shown through my own life what it means to live in accordance with His Will. Yet you and I understand that, if we are to do God's work, we need to ensure our own survival, and have a right to a reasonable degree of comfort. Isaac, on the other hand, seems to have gotten himself so caught up in the experience of reaching out to God through burnt offerings, that he truly believes that he is called on to become such an offering himself. I would prefer to think that my fears are wrong; I dare not.

I am convinced that the God before whom I have walked throughout my adult life cannot abide the widespread pagan practice of human sacrifice. I feel that you share this conviction. Isaac, on the other hand, has cultivated, at his young age, a closeness to the local population. From them he has gained an amazing acquaintance with techniques for working the soil, but he has, in his immaturity, been influenced as well by their fundamental outlook on much else. Thus, just beneath the surface of his consciousness he equates 'most precious possession,' which of course we owe to the Most High, with a human life, his human life. It disturbs me no end to see that his mind fails to see that for a person to so end his own life is equally incompatible with all we believe of our God.

You see the problem. I cannot arbitrarily overrule his deep impulse, if that is truly how he feels. At his age – almost sixteen – he must work this out for himself, but he needs help. Ishmael, in many ways you know him better than I do. Please help us.

Isaac has asked me to travel with him to some secluded spot, as we mark his sixteenth birthday, alone but for the presence of God. Isaac needs some kind of tangible, incontrovertible sign that he is now worthy of being elevated to a higher level of understanding and a more sophisticated expression of commitment. Even more, he must be made to see clearly that 'greater commitment' does not require self-destruction.

Please give this matter the benefit of your thought. I, for one, will know no peace until it is resolved. Should it play out as a tragedy, I will never be able to live with myself. And, should it have a tragic result, it will be the death of Sarah.

I am not sure how fair it is for me to lay this on you, Ishmael. Yet, since from the very beginning you have called Isaac your brother, I feel that I have a right to do so. We dare not fail.

Please give me your ideas.

Your loving Father,

Abraham

ITEM # 242
LETTER FROM ISHMAEL TO ABRAHAM

Dear Father,

I really must thank you for the confidence that you have shown in me, in so many ways.

First of all, the new Southwest Trust. It entails a variety of problems: geographic, commercial, personnel, diplomatic and operational. We have all sorts of good men, and countless contacts, as I am finding out. To forge them into a cohesive and sensibly organized whole is, to say the least, a challenge. I have been working practically around the clock. It will be done!

Your concern for family is being addressed. I am in the process of assembling a family roster. Next comes a master list of our resources – people and logistics – to be broken down into assignment of specific responsibilities. Shortly I will be able to run it by you. (And to think that the challenge of finding water in the Negev once overwhelmed me!) It is fascinating to watch as pieces fall into place.

As to Isaac. I agree with you that he is hard to figure out. In some ways he is more of a spoiled brat than I was at his age. Still, I detect sparks of a spiritual profundity that will always be beyond my power to attain. My correspondence with him reveals that he possesses an almost detached impracticality, and yet he has evaluated all of Canaan's resources in a manner that takes my breath away.

Now that you call it to my attention, Isaac's obsession with self-sacrifice, about which you speak, has surfaced in his letters. To add a touch of irony, he intimates that the idea comes from you. It isn't only that you introduced him to the experience of burnt offerings on an altar. Wasn't it you who taught us to withhold nothing from God?

Father, I am sure you have known all along that there is not much I would refuse to do for Isaac. No question, I will try to save him from this excess of enthusiasm. How do we go about purging his mind of this idea?

I am still trying to master the topography of the Canaan locale just to the north of my territory, and while I have not thought everything through, I have an idea. Think in terms of a mountain where you have not been before, at least not with Isaac. Be careful not to say to Isaac that the trip is for the purpose of giving him back to God as a burnt offering, just describe it as an opportunity to delve more deeply into the concept of sacrifice. I will be there if you need me.

There is more: my Egyptian grandfather, in deference to you, is conscientious in not trying to win me over to actually accepting the validity of the Egyptian system of belief in multiple gods. I, as a dutiful grandson, do go along with him, often with Mother accompanying us, to witness the pomp and pageantry of his religious observances. There is often a bit of the dramatic involved, and you have taught us to learn from everyone. When the moment arrives, I will be able to turn Isaac's mind around.

Again, thanks for your generous confidence in me. We both still remember when we were not sure I could advance to the level of taking out a caravan on my own. If I have been able to come as far as I have, let us both be confident that great things are in store for Isaac. Is that not God's promise?

Your loving son,

Ishmael

ITEM # 243
FILE ENTRY

Memorandum

From: Headquarters, Southwest Trust

To: All Districts

Our new administrator, Ishmael, will shortly embark on an inspection trip of all key stations. You will make certain that any records and documents he might need are available. You will also take care that suitable facilities for uneventful and safe travel are available.

Many of you remember Ishmael as but a lad, and an entry-level trainee. He is now our chief administrator, second only to Abraham. In point of fact, you will be impressed by his comprehensive mastery of a great variety of details as well as by the sweep of his vision.

Attached is a copy of his itinerary, plus a list of what he will wish to be briefed on at each of our stations. He is pleased by the overall picture of the present state of our operations; he now wishes to move forward with 'a plan for tomorrow.' He will be especially interested in your own personal suggestions for future improvements and innovations. This is an opportunity to go outside the chain of command with recommendations, and perhaps even to receive on-the-spot approval.

ITEM # 246
LETTER FROM ABRAHAM TO ISHMAEL

Dear Ishmael,

Things are beginning to come together.

I get reports from all sides of the way in which you have taken hold of the Southwest Trust. It is clear that you have been a 'shadow manager' for some time. Good work!

I am equally impressed with your analysis of Isaac. I realize that I have been underestimating him. Isaac will always be Sarah's 'little boy.' I must be more careful to stop thinking of him as such myself.

The projects I have set for you can be discussed when we manage to have a few days together, but the issue of Isaac's 'burning desire' cannot be put off.

I have done a great deal of soul-searching these past few weeks, and have reached out for Divine guidance. I am confident that what I hear now is God's voice. That Voice calls on me to make a personal decision.

What was I told:

Take Isaac; raise him up to the highest level of Service to Me.

Where?

On a mountain-top. You will know it when you see it.

What happens there?

Abraham, by now I should not have to tell you.

So I am still left with a question which only I can answer: If God tells me, at that moment, 'Sacrifice Isaac,' what do I do?!

There is a city named Shalem, high on a mountain just within the Jebusite border. Its king is called Malki-Zedek. I have not been there often, but from the first, as I entered that area, I was enfolded by a feeling that this is a place special to God and to anyone who wants to experience His presence.

Two days before Isaac's sixteenth birthday we will set out for this mountain. We will make ready, as we have done three times previously, for a 'service of sacrifice.' We will prepare lamb, knife, fire and kindling. Only one thing will be different. We will be providing Isaac with an opportunity to seize this moment to substitute himself as the sacrificial offering.

Will he choose to do so? Very possibly. Can we let that happen? Unless I am mistaken about my God, of course not. To be honest with you, Ishmael, if it turns out that I am in error, if my God will indeed accept a human sacrifice, I will not come down from that mountain.

How do we get through to Isaac? How do we prevent a life from being ended? How do we prevent a human sacrifice and still make this moment for Isaac one of ascending one step closer to God's level? Ishmael, I am counting on you.

You hint that you have some thoughts. I hope to God that they work out. It surely will not be easy.

We should be about two and a half days getting to the Shalem area. There are several mountains clustered together. Moriah, which is not the tallest, has impressive outcroppings of rock. It meets your criterion of being covered with trees. There is where we will be. I expect that we will build an altar and lay out kindling. For that matter, I will look for an excuse to tie Isaac's hands. It will make it that much harder for him to lunge for the knife and do himself some harm.

One more request. I know how difficult this will be for you, but please share my regard for Sarah. I have never been away from Sarah for so long, and she will be worried. She must be satisfied we are alright. You must help us return as quickly as possible.

It is odd, you know. When you turned sixteen, you were the overly protected son of a wealthy man. It took a sequence of traumatic incidents to awaken you to your full potential. Isaac, now, at age sixteen, is the favored son of a man accepted as God's intimate. Now it is he who must be awakened to understanding and reality. You can help in a way that no one else can.

Bring to bear all your ingenuity, your unique perspective, your insight into what makes Isaac tick. Between us, we must manage not to fail Isaac. Between us, we must manage not to fail the One True God, whose rejection of human sacrifice must be made evident to all the world.

In closing, I become again the proud father. There are not too many men who have a son such as you. Any father would be pleased to see his two sons as attached to each other as you are. In all honesty, I sometimes wish Isaac were a little more oriented to the practical, and that you were a bit more directed to the spiritual. No matter, you will each make your mark on the world, and each of you serve the Most High and His plan for the world in your own way.

And each of you is passing an important milestone in his life in this year. Perhaps, I should add, I am as well.

Your loving father,

Abraham

ITEM # 248
LETTER FROM ISHMAEL TO ABRAHAM

Dear Father,

I enjoy being busy, and the past week has been very, very enjoyable. I enjoy even more seeing things fall into place, and since I took over my new duties, life has become a pleasure.

You asked me to look into integrated, expedited point-to-point connections. Well, if you get this letter before you take off with Isaac, you know it works.

My first major project will be a way for you and Isaac to get back to Hebron rapidly from the Moriah mountains. I have to apologize in advance: at this stage, comfort is one element we cannot attend to. But things will get better. I have not compromised on security; speed is, as always, a primary concern.

I should tell you now that the solution includes having our people in position, and with definite assignments, in all useful places, as well as keeping current a list of local people on whom we can call. As so often is the case, the broad outline came from you, but I hope you will agree that I have added a few wrinkles.

You will not see me, but I will know when you leave Hebron. I will know when you arrive at the foot of the mountain. I will know if you light a fire. I will know where the knife is. My hope is that I will know what Isaac is thinking, and understand how to impress him. As I hinted in my last letter – a little bit of drama, a little bit of psychology, and strict attention to timing, should add up to success.

What is left? It would be helpful to be sure we know what God wants. I surely hope we do. Please remember what you taught me, Father: A just God cannot ask us to do what is wrong, and a merciful God calls forth events that work to our good.

Your loving son,

Ishmael

ITEM # 255
FILE ENTRY

Daily Report
* Extract *

From: Security Officer

To: Hebron Operations

As anticipated, Abraham and Isaac, along with their complement of two pack animals, two attendants and assorted supplies, left this morning.

We take note of the fact that Abraham personally supervised the assembly of a choice lamb, kindling, the unusual straight-edged knife and the beautiful firesafe of Ugaritic design.

It is highly disturbing that, after they departed, we detected Abraham's lamb grazing with the flock. A quick head-count showed another lamb gone, but from a flock of the poorest level. We have an uncomfortable feeling that something is brewing; we will get to the bottom of this.

I made a quick decision, and sent out two additional crack scouts commandeered from caravan #7-36, to monitor Abraham and Isaac discreetly. In any event, all our personnel are on alert because, while this is taking place, we are playing host to Ishmael's inspection tour in this general area.

Sarah was up bright and early to kiss Abraham and Isaac good-bye at her tent door. It may be out of our normal area of concern, but she gave a more frail appearance than she has in the recent past.

ITEM # 257
FILE ENTRY

Special Report

From: Security Officer

To: Hebron Operations

Copy To: Administrative Headquarters

It is two days since Abraham and Isaac departed. We are still puzzled by the fact that the animal that was taken with him was not the prime sacrificial animal which he had selected. You may have access to facts that are not available to us.

Whether it was a deliberate substitution by Abraham or some inexcusable error on the part of someone else, the switch has crucial overtones. Today, at noon, Sarah heard from one of her handmaids a story that her husband and son had left for their birthday outing, all prepared for a sacrifice, but minus a sacrificial animal.

To say that Sarah is distraught is putting it mildly. She seems to have come to the conclusion that either Abraham will sacrifice Isaac on the altar, or that he will ask Isaac to sacrifice him. She constantly mutters, 'I should have known.'

She is, of course, our mother. We cannot forbid her to do anything, but we have prevailed on her not to go running in pursuit of Abraham and Isaac. You may wish to provide her with some extra care and companionship.

ITEM # 258
FILE ENTRY

>> Code Red <<
Supplementary Report

From: Security Officer / Hebron

To: Administrative Headquarters

Copy to: Hebron Operations

The fat is in the fire! Since our report of yesterday, a devastating combination of circumstances. First, Sarah, who in spite of her limited physical capabilities cannot be restrained, tracked down one of Isaac's tutors and wormed out of him an incredible account of an adolescent undergoing an identity crisis which manifests itself in his fascination with the idea of offering himself up as a burnt offering to God. Second, she all but forced her way into Abraham's confidential files and discovered a file (of which even we did not know) of correspondence with his son Ishmael.

She puts the two together. One moment, she thinks that Isaac will surely die. A moment later, she is certain that Abraham will die. Next, she suspects that Abraham will have Isaac and Ishmael exchange positions, sacrificing one – or both! Her mood at one moment is rage, at another, sadness. She blames all of us, she blames herself.

This is no longer just a matter of security. We await instructions.

ITEM # 259
FILE ENTRY

Confidential / Urgent

From: Security Officer / Hebron

To: Administrative Headquarters

We are now confident that we have established what happened to the sacrificial lamb that Abraham was to have taken along on his expedition with Isaac. The sheepfold, as all sheepfolds, is continually taking on new people. One of the newest is a rather competent-looking fellow, who turns out to have an Egyptian wife. This would never have caused any second thoughts. Her cousin, he claims, is on the personal staff of Ishmael. These things happen all the time. Seems to have helped him get the job.

The odd part is that we cannot shake him from his story that he was acting on direct instructions from Ishmael in pulling the top quality lamb, personally selected by Abraham, out of the carrier and substituting one of the lowest quality. Incredible as his tale is, it has the ring of truth, but to our analysts it makes no sense. We pass along the information for what it is worth. Perhaps you can connect it up with other information at your disposal.

True or not, understandable or not, it does not change the unfortunate impact on Sarah of the combination of fact and gossip she has been fed. We are afraid staff here is going to have their hands full.

ITEM # 262
FILE ENTRY

Travel Update

From: *Beersheva District Station #3-1*
To: *Hebron District Headquarters*

Ishmael was here early this morning. He seems pleased overall with what he has found along the way. Full details of our meetings will be incorporated into our regular monthly report.

We do wish to advise you that from here he elected to bypass stations #3-2 and #3-3 and to head directly for the Shalem area. Since he is not familiar with the area, we assigned a senior scout to him.

He asked us about any local archery sharpshooters. Fortunately, Kemuel's son Jared was here; I doubt whether there is anyone as good as he outside of Egypt's crack units. (Frankly, to the best of our knowledge, Ishmael himself is unsurpassed.) We could not ask him why, of course, and he volunteered no information. It is strange. We hope that he is not anticipating any trouble – the area has been quiet for years. We took pains to so advise him, and he did not contradict us. Yet, he took Jared along with him.

He also requisitioned double rations for his group. It is probably nothing, but we thought you should know.

ITEM # 264
FILE ENTRY

Field Report

From: Scout Unit #S-3

To: Administrative Headquarters

Abraham's party was turned over to us by Scout Unit #S-1 at dawn of their third day out of Hebron. At about the same time, we made contact with Scout Unit #B-7, functioning as part of Ishmael's inspection team. At the time, we were somewhat surprised, because although the Southwest Trust does indeed extend to the foot of the Shalem mountains, there is really nothing beyond Hebron important enough to be a stop on his inspection trip. We did not think in terms of a family rendezvous, but I get ahead of myself.

Two hours later, we were reinforced by two additional scouts, sent along by Hebron security. They briefed us hurriedly on why they were dispatched. If their chief thinks we can use help, he may be right. It certainly never hurts to be alerted to a potential problem.

Abraham and Isaac, following what we are informed is a familiar pattern, had their two attendants stay at the foot of the peak, named Moriah, along with their pack animals. The attendants gave the sacrificial animal in the carrier a generous watering. On foot and in silence, Isaac shouldering the oversize carrier and a huge bunch of kindling, Abraham carrying a fire safe and a knapsack from which a knife handle protruded, they ascended to an impressive outcropping of rock.

Isaac stopped at a small spring to give the sacrificial lamb one last drink. Even from our distance, we could read surprise on his face.

'Father,' Isaac said, all out of breath, 'it seems strange. Kindling, knife, fire, are as should be. But do you call this a sacrificial lamb! Wherever will we find an acceptable one?'

Abraham looked at the lamb. Hesitantly, his voice barely audible, he whispered, 'Isaac, we will know before long what is pleasing to God.'

They reached the summit. Abraham was grim. Isaac was agitated. Abraham arranged stones into a rough altar. Isaac piled the kindling on top. Then, to our surprise, Abraham tied Isaac's hands in front of him, lifted him bodily, and set him atop the branches.

'Father, what does God want?'

'My son, He wants loyalty, integrity and an understanding heart. He wants love for Him and for all that He has created. He wants us us to reach out to our fellow human beings with compassion and fellowship. He wants devotion to justice. In a word, He wants a lifetime spent in His service.'

'But Father, these are merely words. I hear them, my mind agrees. But doesn't your heart call out for more. Isn't action called for, some tangible, powerful act?'

At that, Isaac lunged for the blade, managed to prop it between his knees, and began to sever the ropes on his wrists. He and Abraham both grappled for the knife; their hands intertwined on the handle. They struggled. Suddenly, their eyes met. They stopped. Our hearts were in our throats.

'Isaac,' said Abraham, 'I hear God's voice.'

'Father,' said Isaac, 'I hear it too.'

Who knows whether they would have gone back to struggling for the knife, or what would have been the outcome, but at that moment an arrow flew by their faces. As they looked in the direction from which the arrow had come, their eyes lit upon a ram, entangled in a thicket, snared by its horns. The sun's rays were reflected from those horns. And, with their four hands still intertwined, they walked over, lifted the ram, and carried it back to the altar.

They looked from the knife to the ram, from the ram to the knife. They slaughtered the ram, and carefully removed its horns. The hornless ram they placed atop the kindling, and made it a symbol of their joint resolve to serve the One God with a fiery passion. And then, with a speed we would have thought impossible, they fashioned one of the horns into a trumpet, and sounded it, as a symbol of their pledge to announce this dedication to God to all the world.

As the flames took hold, and the echo faded, another voice joined theirs. In a moment, Ishmael appeared, and the somber mood gave way to elation. As if by signal, three hands joined, and three faces looked upward, as if looking for God's approval and a Divine blessing. The expression on their faces hinted that they felt it was granted. (I wish I could believe like that.)

Ishmael and his escort unit took over at this point. Any necessary report will have to come from them.

ITEM # 265
LETTER FROM ISHMAEL TO LOCUM-RE

Dear Grandfather,

I had every intention, starting out on my tour of inspection, of concluding it with a brief reunion with my father and brother. Had things gone as I planned, I would have been on my way home by now.

But two things happened. The first, which would have entailed only a minor delay, was the emotional torrent which was released by the Akedah – Isaac being bound as if for a sacrifice – and by the opportunity and challenge it presented. The three of us came face-to-face with questions we had previously looked at alone, reducing them all to the one: What does God want of us?

So right there, on that mountain-top where I swear God gave us a vision of Himself and an insight into what He wants of us, we poured out our hearts to each other. It was a medley of soul-searching and celebration, of unburdening and looking forward. We ate a bit, we drank a bit, but mostly we talked.

We were already winding down the mountain when the second thing happened. It is hard to believe (and I am ashamed to admit it) but none of us had thought of Sarah, and what she might be thinking of Abraham and Isaac's extended absence. A fast rider found us and gave us the message that Sarah had worked herself up into a state of frenzy. She had discovered the Ishmael file in my father's office. Having no news of their return, Sarah was certain that at least one of them was dead.

It took us only moments to decide: the three of us are on our way to Hebron, hopefully to calm Sarah's spirit. I suppose she had to know the truth about me, sooner or later. Since she knows, we must all be with her.

Please help Mother – as well as my own wife and children – understand. I hope to be home soon.

(This letter will reach you via the expedited courier service that I initiated recently. Let me know when it arrives.)

Your dutiful grandson,

Ishmael

ITEM # 266
LETTER FROM SARAH TO TERAH

Dear Father,

In a way, I am relieved, but not fully. Abraham is back. Isaac is back. No one intended to kill anyone (although I still have a lingering unease about Isaac wanting to harm himself). But now, I feel I can never be really certain that your son is not hiding from me things that a husband should share with his wife. I am even less certain that I want to let Isaac out of my sight for more than a few hours.

You will probably get a different slant from Abraham, and perhaps even from Isaac, but let me tell you the events of those five excruciatingly painful days as I see them.

Five days ago this morning, Abraham and Isaac rose before dawn, and tootled off, supposedly to celebrate Isaac's sixteenth birthday on some out-of-the-way hilltop. They were nice enough to stop by my tent to say goodbye, but not a word of what was really in the works. (At this point, you could almost convince me that it would be better if they celebrated like the camel drivers, by getting drunk.) As far as I knew, they would be gone for four days: two days there, an hour or two of prayer, sacrifice and meditation, two days back, and the return around sunset of the fourth day. Then we would have a cozy celebration.

You won't believe what actually happened. They took no suitable sacrificial lamb, as I discovered the next day. Even in retrospect, I am not absolutely convinced that they did not contemplate the possibility of sacrificing either Isaac or Abraham as a burnt offering. At the moment, I certainly did not know what to think. And hard as I press your precious son for a full account of those frightening days, and as hard as he tries to persuade me that the lamb was somehow switched in error, I still come away feeling that he believed God might really ask for Isaac's sacrifice.

When they did not return as planned, it occurred to me that there might be some clue in Abraham's files. I browsed through, and was astounded to find a thick file of correspondence between Abraham and Ishmael, between Abraham and Locum-Re in Zoan (I had been naive enough to think that that connection was all business), and even exchanges between Abraham and Hagar. What would you think? You cannot imagine the thoughts that ran through my mind! Isaac dead. Abraham dead. Ishmael replacing either or both. Hagar replacing me. The vision of the Most High turned sour.

In any case, the staff realized that I had been kept in the dark too long, and that now something had to be done. Fortunately, someone always knows how to reach Abraham, so getting word to him to get back to his wife was only a matter of dispatching an expedited relay. It is impressive to see what they can do if they want to. (Some courier type whom I never saw before implied that they are using a brand new system.)

To make a long story short, the three of them (Abraham, Isaac and Ishmael) showed up just after noon of day five, more than a bit tired. None of us had slept, but we had so much to talk about that it hardly mattered. Don't quote me on this, but Ishmael has turned out to be not a bad sort. His devotion to Isaac, his brother (there, I said it!) is incredible. I love Isaac, and he is touched by a spiritual quality that rivals Abraham's, but he cannot hold a candle to Ishmael in the grasp of practical affairs. That man is a real asset.

But I cannot bear the thought of Isaac running about who knows where. I shall insist that he remain in Hebron at all times. I want him where I can see him every morning and every evening.

Your loving daughter,
Sarah

ITEM # 270
LETTER FROM ELIEZER TO TUBAL

Dear Tubal,

In a way, I have been remiss in not writing to you for a long, long time. It is not because I have been busy, although I have. It is not because we do not trust you to keep a confidence; you long ago proved that you can. The problem is that I cannot sort out events, and what people say and do.

If I live to be four hundred years old, I will never be certain that I have a correct reading on the relationship of Abraham and Ishmael, Abraham and Isaac, Isaac and Ishmael, Sarah and Isaac, Sarah and Ishmael, or – for that matter – Sarah and Abraham. Where Hagar fits in, I don't dare even guess!

I learned quickly enough, that when Abraham pulled Ishmael and Hagar up by the roots, almost on Ishmael's sixteenth birthday, he was actually transplanting them. Little by little, I came to see that Abraham was careful not to disturb Sarah with items of information that would hurt her.

It took a while before it became clear to me that Abraham was sensitively and successfully balancing the needs of Sarah, Isaac, Ishmael, Hagar, and somehow even of Abraham himself.

You know the story. Sarah, physically and emotionally drained by seventy years of waiting, and then the ordeals of childbirth and motherhood. Sarah, whose relationship with Abraham was subtly changed by the birth of Ishmael, and then fundamentally altered by the addition of Isaac and the subtraction of Ishmael. Isaac, the sensitive youngster who has had both too much and too little of his mother. Isaac, who is both the long-awaited 'number one' child and a sort of substitute for the firstborn. Ishmael, for whom Abraham is constantly doing too much, and for whom he can never do enough. Hagar, who was chased away from a 'domestic handmaiden' situation with a package of benefits most people would envy, and who left behind all she ever really wanted.

But my major concern has always been Abraham himself. It was first for him, and only second for his vision of the One Most High God, that I turned my back on what would have been a most satisfying life and rewarding career in Damascus. Abraham has built an amazingly successful commercial enterprise. Abraham has drawn to himself (with the aid of Sarah to be sure) a large collection of people who, to a varying degree, accept his concept of One God, and he has a number of men and women (among whom I am proud to be numbered) who would do anything for him or for his family.

Yet Abraham knows no peace. At the outset, his nephew Lot, adopted as a son, proved to be a disappointment. For much too long, no children. Then a son, Ishmael, with unusual potential, but who eventually proved to lack the one indispensable quality that Abraham's true heir has to have. The belated realization that Sarah, who saw this first and took pains to point it out, was right. The trauma of excising his own son from his household.

Abraham, all the while wrestling with his God and with his comprehension of his God. Abraham, step-by-step learning about devotion, about justice, about love, about family, about loyalty, about sacrifice, about community and about continuity.

Take this final test. This adolescent of an Isaac, having convinced himself that he was called on to be served up as a burnt offering, bursting to find an opportunity to do so. Abraham, out of a lifetime of getting to know God better and better, sensing that the One True God cannot desire human sacrifice, yet not able to resist Isaac's determination and enthusiasm. Abraham, not positive beyond the shadow of a doubt that Isaac's call is anything but authentic. Abraham, all but sure that he will manage to sway

Isaac, not telling Sarah of the plans. Abraham, admitting in his heart that there is always the possibility that Isaac will not return, and knowing that in that case he too will not return. Abraham, calling out to Ishmael for help. Ishmael, who would never say no with his brother involved, answering his father's call with a 'Here I am.'

Finally, Sarah, almost pushed over the edge by all this.

Anyway, there was, you realize, no sacrifice of Isaac, but things are not the same. After that experience, everyone seems to discount the possibility of Isaac marrying and having children. Strange.

Actually, Tubal, that may work out to my advantage. All the pieces are not yet in place, but while he must wind up with a senior position in the Four Rivers Trading Company, I sense the unlikelihood that the top spot will go to Ishmael. (Did I tell you that he came to Hebron with Abraham and Isaac, and Sarah greeted him like a long-lost cousin?) At the very least, someone will have to run the Damascus-Hebron and/or the Damascus-Ur segments. If things pan out, and especially if Isaac has no children, one of those spots will be mine. Let us both look into it. And if you can, find out what is doing in Ugarit; I could develop that as my own.

I hope I have not gotten you needlessly confused. By now, I think we are down to the normal stresses of daily living. About time, I say.

Your cousin,

Eliezer

ITEM # 273
LETTER FROM ABRAHAM TO TERAH

Dear Father,

I had thought, when I originally took up residence just outside the lovely settled city of Hebron, that I would never be moving again. It does not seem to be working out that way.

It has to do with Ishmael. It took me a long time to erase from my mind the image of a lad whose failure almost cost him and his mother their lives when they had to make their way from Canaan to Egypt. He came up short in initiative, resourcefulness and nerve. I kept getting reports of his maturation, but, even when I installed him as head of the new Southwest Trust, I still retained a picture of the eternal child who would fail in the clutch. It has taken this business with Isaac and the aborted sacrifice to show me that I can truly rely on Ishmael.

I went along with Isaac, in deed and in thought, on that terrifying trip. You could have described me as teetering on the brink of insanity. I was full of second thoughts about Isaac and his stability, and I was in a quandary as to what God really wanted. In spite of being morally certain that He cannot desire a human sacrifice, I was (and still am) beset by the question of how far we can go, may go, must go in obedience to a Voice seeming to emanate from On High. My underlying doubt, about Ishmael, tied all the doubts together into one package wrapped in confusion and uncertainty.

Then I discovered the new Ishmael. I conveyed to him the gist of the problem, and he figured out the rest. Maneuvering things so that what we had with us was an absolutely unacceptable lamb, devising a way to substitute a ram for the lamb by planting it in the thicket, getting our attention with an arrow shot across our brows (He says he did not shoot it; he is my son, I have to believe him.) from that precise direction – all this added up to what was needed to force us to think again, and to think more clearly. I will never sell Ishmael short again.

Ishmael, for all that he is now on speaking terms with Sarah, really cannot be tolerated in the same household with her. Neither one of them is ready for that, if ever they will be. Sarah is certainly not about to accept the presence of his wife, or of anyone's wife, as a second matron in the household. Besides, he has created for himself quite a comfortable life in the heart of the Paran wilderness. Since I feel a need to be closer to him than I have been, and since wilderness and I are no longer compatible, I have picked out a lovely homestead near the well of Beersheva, where we have quite an efficient and pleasant team in place.

I am not certain what Sarah will do. Knowing why I want to relocate, she is not quite comfortable with the idea of moving. Additionally, she is comfortable here and does not want to start anew. Probably she will continue to reside in Hebron – really Kiryat Arba – and spend a little bit of time in Beersheva. I will most likely spend more time in Beersheva and the regions to the south, while Isaac will bear most of the burden of taking care of his mother. It should work out.

I close by again extolling the virtues of this lovely land of Canaan. In every conceivable way, it is God's country. And every day, young Isaac, whom I faulted for going off on endless wanderings, finds fresh spots of beauty, and dreams up original ways of creating new visions of loveliness. He is indeed the one to inherit the land. He will make it ours.

Sarah, you will be happy to learn, is a bit stronger than she has been for quite some time. For the first time in recent memory, I have lost the fear that any given week or month will be her last.

So my world is more complete now than it has been for a long time – maybe ever. It is as if the acts of faith that might have cost us so dearly have proved to be vehicles for God's blessing.

Your contented son,

Abraham

ITEM # 289
LETTER FROM ISAAC TO ISHMAEL

Dear Ishmael,

One of Father's managers is fond of saying, 'We live from day to day.' It may be true for some people; I live from problem to problem.

You were on hand thirteen years ago when Father and I together came to see once and for all that God absolutely rejects the idea of human sacrifice. Together, we three began to grapple with finding a definitive answer to the question of what He really wants of us. (I am not now naive enough to think you just happened to come by on your tour of inspection.)

Those few days turned my life around. I saw the folly of my determination to become fuel for the flames of a fiery altar. Just as happened to you at the same age, I grew up and started directing my energy and my reading and studies to one central purpose. In my case, it was towards defining settled and established life on the land. It did not take me long to realize that this had been in me all along. There is much that I have always had trouble remembering, but I never forgot any location where Father successfully dug for water. Actually, I can even pinpoint most of the spots where he dug for water and came up dry. Don't tell Father that I said this, but I think that right now I know things about farming and about animal husbandry that he does not know. God promised this land to Father and those who come after him, and I am determined to make it ours in every way.

So what is the problem? You (I admit this freely) will understand more than anyone else when I say the problem is my Mother, Sarah. She loves me, to be sure, but with an unnatural intensity. She does not let me out of her sight! If she had her way, I would be with her for breakfast, lunch and dinner. She all but tucks me into bed at night. I know why, of course. In her mind she is just making sure that I don't one day decide again to sacrifice myself. Father, of course, has no choice but to let her have her way. (Would you agree that this has always been so?)

For a long time, marriage has been on my mind. Yet, for all practical purposes, it is out of the question. I don't have to explain to you that the idea of any woman coming in here to share in our lives would simply destroy her emotionally, and perhaps physically as well. So I can neither take even a short trip (much less one as far as Kharran) to select a wife, or have a woman come here to be my bride.

I compensate by keeping busy. There is much to do here. Through normal administrative channels, you will soon be receiving detailed information about new agricultural products to add to your catalogue, including higher quality wool.

A final note. I know you have sources of information about the Philistines. Please get their charts of underground water. I also hear they have developed new techniques and materials for producing weaponry. Try to find out what they are doing, if anything, to develop better plows and harvesting equipment.

My fondest regards to your wife and children.

With brotherly affection,

Isaac

ITEM # 293
LETTER FROM ISHMAEL TO ISAAC

Dear Isaac,

You do not have to tell me how busy you have been. I hear reports of your activities and your successes from all sides.

The new strains of grain you have added to our inventory have been extremely well received. People are already attempting to adapt one or two of them to Egypt; they will get no help from me. I suggest that you keep your research a secret as well. I am trying to follow up on a rumor that somewhere around the second cataract of the Nile they are harvesting fifty to sixty measures of grain from one measure of seed and are now shooting for one hundred. Can you believe it? You know, without my telling you, that these things are closely guarded secrets.

There are secrets of all kinds in this world of ours. The Philistines can be very friendly and sweet when they want to be, or when they think you might tell them something they want to know. But try to pry some information out of them, and they become as silent as the grave. The reply that one always receives when asking them about the manufacture of swords or axes, or for that matter plows, is: 'Tell us what you need; we can sell you anything.' They can – and do!

When it comes to water, they are worse. Not only is it next to impossible to worm out of them any information about sources of water; they act as if any water around is their exclusive property. They sense that the supply of water is not limitless and they go so far as to close down any well which does not meet with their approval. You will have to get to know them, but they will not be easy to deal with.

What do you people hear from Grandpa Terah and the others in Kharran and Ur? Setting up contacts outside the Southwest Trust territory has not yet happened – the farthest I have gotten my people to is Megiddo. Check it out with Eliezer; that man must know more than his official duties require. Don't ask him outright, but I am sure he has kept active his contacts in all directions from Damascus.

What I am driving at is, neither of us has actually met Grandpa, and I would love to set up a get-together. Maybe your mother could help us figure something out. We would have to promise not even to look at his idols. (Between you and me, the ones that get to Egypt are works of art, but we don't need a repetition of the grief they once caused us.)

Meanwhile, if you can get down here I would be happy to show you areas of vegetation that seem to thrive on little water. Perhaps there are plant strains you can use. Hopefully, Sarah will find your absence on a trip of that duration tolerable. I, for one, would love to see you.

With brotherly affection,

Ishmael

ITEM # 298
LETTER FROM NAHOR TO ABRAHAM

Dear Abraham,

I know your new mail system has its successes. I see from time to time letters coming from Sarah and you, mostly to Father. Anyway, this caravan leader assured me that a letter from me can get to a friend in Hamath, from him to a business contact in Damascus, thence to a trusted person in Megiddo, and then on to you before the next moon. I'll try anything once. You will let me know if it gets to you.

First, the good news. I am sure you know that Milkah and I have been blessed with children, eight in number. Our youngest, Betuel, now has a son, Laban, and a daughter, Rebecca. She is cute, clever and good-hearted. If you ask me (as an unbiased grandfather!), she is too good for the crude types around here.

I understand that Ishmael has given you grandchildren. What is happening with Isaac? I hear good things about him, but not a single word about a wife or children.

By the way, once in a long while we used to meet a fantastic fellow who joined up with you, from Damascus I think. Whatever became of him?

The other news is about Father. He has slowed down quite a bit, which is not surprising, since he is getting on to two hundred years of age. He loves your letters and the occasional note from a grandson, but he misses you. Actually, the one he misses most is Sarah. As you know, she bears an amazing resemblance to her mother, and now that she has died (I assume that Father told you) he finds it hard to be separated from Sarah. The other day he surprised me by saying, 'Maybe I should have gone on to Canaan with Sarai and Abram.' (He keeps forgetting your name changes.)

I hope this last point does not upset you too much; I felt that you ought to know.

Milkah and I send our best to Sarah and to you.

Your brother,

Nahor

ITEM # 300
FILE ENTRY

Administrative Order

From: Abraham

To: All Units

This will officially confirm what many of you already know concerning the role of Isaac in the organization.

Isaac is hereby delegated prime responsibility for three operational areas:

1. Agriculture
2. Livestock management
3. Water resources

Included, as a matter of course, are any issues relating to food production.

Management of food stocks and addressing food shortages are the joint responsibility of Isaac and Ishmael.

(Any related transportation questions will continue to be referred to Ishmael.) Isaac's headquarters will be situated in Hebron, with a field office in Beersheva.

Reports clearly requiring his personal attention will be directed to him in Hebron. Routine matters, as always, are to be transmitted to Administrative Headquarters.

ITEM # 289
LETTER FROM ISAAC TO ISHMAEL

Dear Ishmael,

It is my sad duty to pass on to you the sad news of two deaths. Mother's mother passed away a short time ago, and just now Father's mother has died. Neither was young, but Father and Mother have taken the news quite hard. The fact that they had not seen them for so long made it strike home that much harder.

Mother, of course, is in no physical condition to go see her father, Grandpa Terah. Father will not take such a long trip without her. For me to leave for such an extended time, even for this reason, is out of the question. Can I impose on you to test your plans for a long-distance caravan ride by going on one yourself?

Father would not ask you to expose yourself to such rigors, and it is probably brash of me to ask you, but it would do wonders for Grandpa. Frankly, you are the only one around who has had the experience of talking to a grandfather. You cannot deny that a firsthand report would provide a boost for Father and Mother.

Ishmael, I hope you can do it.

Fondly,

Isaac

ITEM # 306
LETTER FROM ISHMAEL TO LOCUM-RE

Dear Grandfather,

You have no idea what a thrill it was for me to meet my other grandfather, Terah, for the first time. I was nervous at the prospect of such a lengthy trip; it was a sort of test of our theories and innovations in long-distance travel. I must say that I was proud of all my people.

I was more than a little uneasy about meeting Terah, about whom I had heard so much, but whom I had never met. The family put me completely at ease. Betuel and Milkah are marvelous hosts. On the other hand, watching them both basking in what is to me the luxury of seeing parents, children, brothers and sisters every day makes me realize what I have been missing. At least I have Mother and you.

Much as I was overjoyed to see Grandpa, it pained me to see Terah so visibly old. I now have the difficult job of giving an honest report to Father and Sarah. If I can, I will delegate part of the task to Isaac. The fact that he has been so close to his mother just might make it easier.

Do you want to hear something cute? Betuel's youngest daughter, Rebecca, is quite precocious. She really floored me by asking, first, whether I am married, next whether I believe in a man taking more than one wife (I think she was disappointed that I said yes) and finally, whether Isaac is married. I think it best not to report that conversation in full to Isaac. Perhaps I will take the easy way out and delegate that tidbit to Father. He has the gift of handling touchy situations. Heaven knows he has had enough of them!

You know who else is getting old: trusty Eliezer. We must force ourselves to realize that he has been with Father almost sixty years, and that he was a man of great experience even before they met. There are still missions that Father would entrust to no one else. His advice is rarely off the mark. Still and all, I sense (even if Father does not) that he is slowing down. I would love to see Father come up with one more major assignment to give him the opportunity to shine, and then find him a quiet retirement spot near Damascus.

Father, on the other hand, is absolutely amazing. He has the enthusiasm and vitality of a much younger man. Too bad things are so different for Sarah!

Even though I now will be taking time out to give firsthand reports to Abraham and Sarah, I should manage to get back to Egypt for the next Zoan District meeting. Is there anything you want me to bring you?

Your loving grandson,

Ishmael

ITEM # 309
LETTER FROM NAHOR TO ABRAHAM

Dear Abraham,

It was quite a pleasure seeing your son Ishmael. He is such a mixture of qualities that I could never begin to describe him to someone who does not know him. He endeared himself to everyone here.

He did so much more. He gave all of us, especially Father, an insight into a variety of things that we had only second-hand knowledge of before his visit. Hearing him present a detailed, personal account of those trying days when his mother and he left your household and wound up in Egypt, and his enumeration of the supports that were put quietly in place for them, made me burst with pride at your ingenuity. I was even more proud of the way in which he adapted himself to unfortunate circumstances. Listening to his 'observer's report' of the events at the top of Mount Moriah made me feel that I was holding both Isaac and you by the hands as you endured that hushed climb up the slope.

What was most touching and – considering the personal dynamics – most considerate, was his report on why Sarah could not make the trip, and why it was necessary for you and Isaac to stay behind to be close to her. We are truly sorry that you could not be here with us.

It grieves me to have to convey to you the sad information that this was the last opportunity to see Father Terah. I supposed that he willed himself to stay alive long enough to see at least one of your children. He quietly slipped away about a week ago, and was laid to rest in the midst of the grove of trees that so endeared Kharran to him almost eighty years ago. He lived a full life of two hundred and five years, and his only disappointment was in not having a son to take over his idol-making business. (For all that, I like to think that he was proud of both of us and of our respective accomplishments.)

By the way, it is years since we have heard anything from or about Lot. If you have a way of reaching him, please tell him about Father. Through the grapevine, we have heard that he had two married daughters, and a couple of grandchildren. Beyond that, nothing.

By the way, Ishmael's visit proved that travel from one area to another is not so difficult any longer. We must find a way to be in touch more frequently. I have a growing family, you have a growing family. (Ishmael was sort of hazy in his details about Isaac.) They ought to know each other.

One final item – ask Ishmael to give you his impressions of my granddaughter Rebecca. In many ways, she reminds me of Sarah at her age.

Your loving brother,

Nahor

ITEM # 321
LETTER FROM ABRAHAM TO LOCUM-RE

Dear Locum-Re,

No matter how well we think that we are prepared for the inevitable, it is always a shock when it comes.

You know, of course, that I am talking about the death of my beloved Sarah. We had one hundred and nine years of sharing. Whatever I may have accomplished in life would have been impossible without her. She traveled willingly, first to Kharran, (where she would have loved to remain with Father, to whom she was very close), then to northern Canaan, then to Hebron, briefly to Egypt, where we met you, then back to Hebron to stay. She never wavered in her devotion to the One God, and she always shared enthusiastically in the vision of spreading word of Him far and wide. Towards the end, she came around to accepting my constant attachment to Ishmael, and my confidence in him as a senior partner in the Four Rivers Trading Company.

Sarah possessed a capacity for deepfelt passion, and intense emotional attachment. This depth of feeling bound us together, body, mind and spirit. She was the ideal partner. At the same time, she loved Isaac with an extraordinary, almost possessive sort of intensity. And finally, she had a high regard for her father, Terah, that I appreciated only towards the end.

For the last thirty-seven or thirty-eight years, since the arrival of Isaac on the scene, her health has been precarious, but we had gotten used to frequent crises and had come to expect her to pull out of them. So, when she started going downhill after the news of Father's death, we expected her to come back to herself once again. When she did not, when I realized that no miracle was going to save her, it hit me with a force I just cannot describe. I wept uncontrollably for days. I was actually in Beersheva when the end came.

Isaac was a tower of strength. I realize now that forcing me to make the funeral arrangements was the best thing he could have done for me. He was the one who suggested the Machpelah caves nearby. (He is quite certain of the authenticity of a local legend that it is the final resting place of the first human couple.) Having to sit down and deal with Ephron and that gang of Hittites brought me back to the world of reality.

Ishmael showed once again his knack for being around, but discreetly. He was a great support when the crowd of comforters finally dissipated. And it was he who eventually prodded me into the realization that it is high time that we go about finding Isaac a wife.

I have been mulling over details. I will be calling on the advice and active help of my 'old dependable' Eliezer (you remember him, no doubt) for one last project. He has never failed me yet. And then, with that worry off my mind, I will finally be able to relax and enjoy life.

My best to all your family, especially Hagar.

As ever,

Abraham

ITEM # 324
LETTER FROM ELIEZER TO TUBAL

Dear Tubal,

I am somewhat old to be talking of a milestone in my life, but I cannot think of a better word for what is going to be happening. I will preface what I have to tell you by repeating an expression that I have heard from Abraham many times: Events take their course, and for the moment we are surprised at how they have turned out. Then, as we think about it, we realize that we knew all along what was destined to happen.

Within a month after Sarah died, almost a year ago, Abraham faced up to the fact that he had seen her failing for some time, and had sensed that her days were numbered. Again, within an hour of Ishmael's voicing the opinion that it was about time to find a mate for Isaac, Abraham admitted to himself and to us that the idea had been in the back of his mind even while Sarah was still clinging to life.

Why do I mention this: you know as well as I do that almost as far back as I can remember, I have had hopes that I would some day inherit the magnificent organization that Abraham has created, with my modest assistance. There were moments when even Abraham was almost ready to concede that no one better would appear on the horizon. But that was more than fifty years ago. When Ishmael was born, Abraham accepted him as his heir almost immediately.

It is simple poetic justice, then, that my final assignment from Abraham was to look up 'the bride' for Isaac and to check her out. I like to think that the way in which I orchestrated it bordered on the brilliant. All the indicators pointed in one direction: Rebecca. She is from the 'old home,' from the right family. Rebecca is pretty, forthright, spunky and intelligent. Abraham and I concluded, though, that we were a little short on any testimonial as to her character. The purpose of my mission, then, was to test her.

Tubal, I have finally admitted to myself that deep down I wanted Rebecca to fail the test. There must have been a soft spot inside my brain that reasoned that if a suitable bride were not found for Isaac now, he would never marry, he would not inherit, somehow it would all come my way. Realistically, it could not have happened, but, to be honest, I suppose that when I prayed to Abraham's God as I entered the Kharran area, I was almost asking Him to help my mission to fail.

You have heard of the test that I set up. The young lady, to qualify, had to offer on her own to draw water for the camels and personnel of a large, thirsty entourage. Nine thousand, nine hundred and ninety-nine young ladies would have failed that test. My luck – Rebecca was the unique, perfect number ten thousand who proved beyond a doubt that, in addition to her other qualities, she also possesses the soul of generosity. The privilege of really getting to know her on the trip home made the final assignment of my career the most enjoyable one of a long lifetime of service.

Then, arriving home in Beersheva, the crowning touch: 'love at first sight.' It was heartwarming: seeing Isaac and Rebecca united in marriage, being treated to the sight of Isaac carrying his bride over the threshold of the tent that had been his mother's, seeing Abraham beaming with joy, knowing that there is now once again a lady of the manor.

I am truly happy that I had a share in making this come about. Now, it is time to go on to a newer and quieter existence. When I see you, before too long, we will have to find a way to keep me busy – but not too busy.

Your cousin,

Eliezer

ITEM # 336
FILE ENTRY

Personnel Action

From: Administrative Headquarters

To: Senior Personnel

Eliezer, confidential assistant to Abraham and administrator at large, is assigned as senior adviser to the Damascus field office. He is the ranking resident in the Hamath district. Even though he is not officially part of your team, you may feel free to ask for his guidance from time to time. You may rely on his advice, when and as given; however budgetary deliberations and routine matters will follow existing administrative procedure. Take care not to overburden him with too many problems.

He will be drawing a pension directly from this headquarters. Additionally, however, he is authorized to call on you for funds and material assets to meet any and all personal needs. Accountability will be referred to this Headquarters.

ITEM # 337
FILE ENTRY

Confirmation of Status

From: Administrative Headquarters

To: All Senior Personnel

Rebecca, wife of Isaac, has taken her place as the mistress of the household and of all related affairs.

In the normal course of events, all her needs will be provided for as part of the daily operation of the Hebron and/or Beersheva residences. Should she, however, make any request of you, you are directed to comply without question.

In due course, she will accompany Isaac on tours of inspection throughout the extended area. You will be apprised of details when and as appropriate.

ITEM # 340
FILE ENTRY

Certificate of Appointment

From: Abraham

To: All Staff

Effective immediately, operational leadership of the Four Rivers Trading Company, including, but not limited to, commercial, transportation, agricultural and all allied activities, is vested in Isaac.

He is also charged with carrying on the mission of communicating at large the vision of the One Most High God.

We expect that he will continue to take a personal interest in agricultural activity and, to a somewhat lesser extent, management of water resources, rather than delegate them. You will hear from him directly.

My new bride, Keturah, and I will always be happy to receive you in our new home, and will be pleased to introduce you to our growing family.

ITEM # 354
FILE ENTRY

Reorganization Plan

From: Administrative Headquarters

To: All concerned

Effective immediately, Abraham is retired from active leadership of the Four Rivers Trading Company. Any questions to him should be routed through Isaac.

Also effective immediately, Isaac's title is Managing Director of the Four Rivers Trading Company. Isaac will continue to personally supervise all research and development in the fields of agriculture, animal husbandry and water resource management.

Ishmael assumes the new position of Senior Operations Officer. He retains prime responsibility for caravans and other transport, for maintenance of oases and like facilities and for commercial arrangements. He will oversee routine day-to-day operations.

Fuller details, as well as the roster of assignments to specific operations and locations, will be published in an updated manual of operations.

ITEM # 355
FILE ENTRY

Clarification of Eligibility

From: Administrative Headquarters

To: All Personnel

Pursuant to special arrangements arrived at by Abraham, a number of individuals, including concubines and offspring, and others related to Abraham, will now be officially recognized as 'correspondents.'

(1) Such individuals will be issued, and will carry at all times, an accepted form of identification.

(2) Such individuals have the right to call on you for routine courtesies, emergency response and humane assistance. They are authorized access to non-classified information in our possession.

(3) In the spirit of mutuality, such individuals consent to be approached with requests for similar courtesies and information.

(4) Said individuals shall be shown preference, where practical, in all commercial endeavors carried on by you.

A Final Note...

ITEM # 360
LETTER FROM YOVAV TO ELIEZER

Dear Eliezer,

We all realize that at your age, and in your physical condition, an expedited trip from Damascus to pay your last respects to Abraham would have been too arduous, but obviously you are entitled to a full report of his funeral.

I personally saw to it that the news of Abraham's death reached you by the speediest means available, as quickly as we notified the people in Kharran and Ur. Both Isaac and Ishmael, who themselves have taken his death hard, have asked me to convey to you their sympathy. They are concerned, considerate individuals, and it would have been a pleasure for you to work under them.

Abraham, as you know better than I, was always able to make his feelings and wishes known. He had made it amply clear to all of us that he wished to be laid to rest next to Sarah, his wife of one hundred and nine years, in the Machpelah cave in the city of Hebron. For Isaac, it was the most natural thing; for Ishmael to bury his father next to a woman other than his mother (and other than his present wife, Keturah) must have been soul-wrenching. Yet, things went smoothly, mainly thanks to the wonderfully full, deep, unconditional brotherly understanding between Ishmael and Isaac.

This closeness was apparent to all of us in the way in which they had monitored Abraham's failing health rather closely for several months. The last few days of his life they spent together at his side. Between them, Abraham was not alone for any time at all from about three days before his death until the interment was completed. Fortunately, they were spared the negotiations for a burial site that the family had to go through when Sarah died.

Among the many tributes to this great man, both Ishmael and Isaac spoke lovingly of their father. It was touching the way these two tributes complemented one another. A couple of our 'dear friends' who look for such things were disappointed not to be able to pounce on any evidence of resentment for certain acts of their father that may have upset them.

They led the procession to the graveside, walking shoulder to shoulder. Next came Abraham's widow Keturah. (We have been given to understand that no one is to remark at her close resemblance to Hagar, mother of Ishmael, and at the close proximity of her new residence to the Paran area, where Ishmael established his headquarters. But if there is anything to know, you must know it.)

Abraham was carried in a most loving fashion by six of his grandsons: Nevaiot, Kedar, Adbe'el and Mivsam, and Isaac's twins, Esau and Jacob. (I cannot believe that they are already fifteen years old.) Mahalat, though not Ishmael's oldest grandchild, took personal charge of a team that made sure that no one lacked for food or other necessities during the days immediately before and after. Forgive me if I note that Mahalat gave a great amount of attention to her cousin Esau – they do make a fine couple.

Isaac did add something on his own: He converted the stark simplicity of the Machpelah cave into a tomb of breathtaking beauty, as a fitting tribute to his two parents. It was conceived, designed and made ready for public view in the space of thirty days. Is it true that he did not always impress people as being quite practical?

Eliezer, I have observed Isaac, and for that matter Ishmael as well. I am supremely confident that Abraham's insights and teachings will not be lost. Yet, in a very real sense, an era has come to a close. I was not with Abraham nearly as long as you, but it was long enough to make me realize, as you did instinctively from the start, that Abraham was a most unusual man. Possibly the world will never again know such a person. We might find many ways to describe his greatness, but on one thing we would agree, and I am certain that the world will agree: He changed forever the way in which we think of God and of the relationship of human beings to God.

This, I am certain, will be his true, lasting memorial.

I have succeeded, my dear colleague and friend, before my own retirement becomes effective, in remedying one significant omission. We shared the intuition when you left, that the time was not right for you to ask permission to make personal copies of items in the file in which you had a legitimate interest. So you left without any of them. The appropriate time did come. Isaac, Ishmael, Rebecca and Ishmael's wife were in my office together, looking for a copy of some record of eighty years ago. I was able to put my hand on it, and remarked how good a system you had for everything. Rebecca reminisced about the sweet man who brought her from Kharran to Canaan. It was the easiest thing for me to remark on what it would mean for you to have a few copies of this and that. On the spot, I was authorized to have copies made of anything in the files that I think you might want to have. They did more, they unlocked for me Abraham's, Sarah's and their own personal files, and said, 'Take anything. It was his work that created it all.' Most generous. It was Ishmael who took me aside and said, 'If you find three or four items that you think he would want no one to see, remove them.' I actually found seven; the originals that I include here are the only copies.

What I am sending you is a sizable bundle, well over three hundred items in all. (Knowing me, you will not be surprised that I have numbered everything. Retain the numbers or not as you see fit.) A page here and there you will choose to destroy. A large part, I am sure, you will elect not to keep. It is for you to decide what is of importance to you. But when the day is done, you will have a more comprehensive record of Abraham's years than exists in any other one place.

They were in such a good mood, that I was inspired to ask for their generosity in providing for my own retirement. They were liberal beyond my most optimistic expectations. Megiddo, here I come!

Thanks again, Eliezer, for trusting me to work with you so closely in caring for Abraham's archives. The three of us worked well together. Now younger hands will take over.

Respectfully yours,

Yovav